101
WILD
THINGS
Along the Grand Strand

Text and Photos by James Luken
Photos by Richard Moore

PCF*Press*

Edited by Amy Godenick.
Design and layout by Susan Jones Ferguson.
All photos unless otherwise noted by Richard Moore.
Project management by Yon Lambert.
Text copyright © 2005 by James Luken and Richard Moore.
Published by Palmetto Conservation Foundation
PCF Press
PO Box 1984
Spartanburg, SC 29304
www.palmettoconservation.org

10 09 08 07 06 05 04 03 02 01

Printed in the United States.

ISBN 0-9745284-4-7

Library of Congress Cataloging-in-Publication Data has been applied for.

Acknowledgments

John Thieret (Northern Kentucky University) reviewed the entire manuscript and made many helpful comments. Eric Wright (Coastal Carolina University) designed the map of the Grand Strand. Coastal Carolina University supported many aspects of this project. The following individuals and organizations provided photographs. Don Millus (croaker fishing), Steve Smith (beavers), Rob Young (bottlenose dolphin), Fritz Rohde (flathead catfish), Reginald Daves (sanderling and willet), Dan Abel (sharks), M. Scott Harris (Carolina Bay), Huntington Beach State Park (loggerhead sea turtle), USPHS Centers for Disease Control and Prevention (mosquito and tick), Freestockphotos.com (black bear).

NORTH
MYRTLE
BEACH

N

90

Wacammaw R.

17

Atlantic
Ocean

501   CONWAY   MYRTLE
BEACH

544

701

17

GEORGETOWN

Winyah Bay

miles

10   20   30

Contents

Introduction

The Grand Strand is a tourist mecca attracting millions of people very year. Most of these people come here to enjoy the beaches, the restaurants, the shopping, the entertainment, and the nightlife. Indeed, these are the things that defined Myrtle Beach when the first hotel was built in 1901 and these are things that define the Grand Strand today. However, the Grand Strand is also recognized for its great variety of natural features. For many visitors and new residents, the animals and plants they encounter are unfamiliar and strange. The extensive marshes, rivers, swamps, and forests appear uninviting and mysterious. As such, nature is not often a part of a visit to the Grand Strand. The purpose of this book is to help visitors and new residents experience and enjoy some of the common wild places and things that occur in this unique coastal area of South Carolina.

A Brief Sketch of the Area

The Grand Strand is informally defined as the coastal area extending south from Little River to Georgetown. In this book, we expand the informal concept of the Grand Strand to include areas from the beach west to the Waccamaw River. It is roughly 60 miles from the northern end of the Grand Strand to the southern end. Distances from the beach to the Waccamaw River vary greatly depending on what road or path is taken. Conway, located on the Waccamaw River, is about 15 miles from the beach. U.S. 501 marks the midsection of the Grand Strand, the first major road built for travel from Conway to the beach, as well as the widest section of the Grand Strand (15 miles). Visitors traveling to the north end of the Grand Strand from Conway usually take SC 90 and end up in Little River Neck. Visitors traveling to the south end of the Grand Strand from Conway usually take SC 544 as the preferred route for linking up with U.S. 17 bypass.

Within the Grand Strand, water determines the types of natural communities and it also often determines the development patterns that give rise to human communities. Several aquatic and wetland areas are noteworthy.

Bald Cypress trees line much of the Waccamaw River.

The Waccamaw River. Originating at Lake Waccamaw in North Carolina and ending at Winyah Bay, this black water river supports a tremendous variety of organisms and habitats. Tides influence the flow of water. Associated communities include floodplain forests, freshwater wetlands, abandoned rice fields, and brackish marshes. Development along the Waccamaw has been sparse due to a paucity of high ground.

Recreational boating now dominates the ICW.

The Atlantic Intracoastal Waterway (ICW). The ICW was originally conceived in the early 1900's as a superhighway for commercial boat traffic. A section of the ICW stretches the entire length of the Grand Strand. In the southern part of the Grand Strand the ICW follows the path of the Waccamaw River. However, in the northern part of the Grand Strand the ICW is an excavated canal. Recreational boaters now dominate this waterway, while upscale homes line the shore.

Salt marshes like these are the nurseries of the ocean.

Inlets and salt marshes. An inlet is a small channel that allows seawater to flow into salt marsh systems existing behind barrier islands. Inflow occurs on a rising tide. Inlets also allow water to flow out of salt marshes on a falling tide. Inlets serve as important migration routes for people and aquatic organisms. From the north to the south, major Grand Strand inlets include Little River Inlet, Hog Inlet, Murrells Inlet, and North Inlet. The shorelines of salt marshes are lined with houses; however, almost every Grand Strand salt marsh includes some protected area.

The distinctive oval shape of Carolina Bays is best viewed from the air.

Carolina Bays. These are shallow, oval-shaped depressions that now form major wetland systems along the Grand Strand. Most Carolina Bays support dense shrub vegetation although some bays have open water in the middle. Carolina Bays are important habitats for large mammals, amphibians, reptiles, and rare plants. Most Carolina Bays have been altered by drainage and encroachment by development at the edges.

Swamps along the Grand Strand are black water systems.

Swamps. Slow-moving water in small creeks flows toward the Waccamaw River. Forested swamps with baldcypress and red maple trees develop around most of these creeks. Many roads along the Grand Strand cross named swamps (e.g., Tilley swamp passing under S.C. 90). Swamps are protected as wetlands, but development around swamps may be changing water quality.

Some storm water detention ponds are high-quality habitats for birds, reptiles and amphibians.

Stormwater detention ponds. Subdivisions and commercial developments in the Grand Strand are associated with hundreds of small constructed ponds. These are required by law to temporarily hold back stormwater rushing from roads and parking lots during heavy rains. Stormwater detention ponds provide habitat for many types of plants and animals. Interestingly, stormwater detention ponds, if constructed correctly, can improve water quality as pollutants are removed by various biological and physical processes.

With the exception of sand dunes adjacent to the beach, most of the terrestrial areas along the Grand Strand are forested. Forest types vary depending on elevation, soil, water availability, and proximity to ocean. Good examples of maritime forests with live oaks still exist in a few spots along the beach. However, most forests in this region are mixtures of pines (loblolly and slash pines) and hardwoods (sweetgum, oaks, and red maple) representing the trees that grew back after the last logging event. Pine plantations can be recognized by the lack of hardwoods and the regular spacing of the pine trees. It is common for real estate developers to thin the forest leaving widely spaced pine trees. Such forests, if not immediately developed, will eventually support a dense understory of vines, shrubs, and resprouting trees. Old beach ridges and the rims of Carolina Bays can be identified by the presence of bleached sand, stunted turkey oaks and the occasional longleaf pine.

Maritime forests contain a mixture of deciduous and evergreen trees as well as palmettos like this.

Forces of Change

Longleaf pine forests require frequent fire.

Fires, hurricanes, and humans are the major factors that have for many years shaped the Grand Strand landscape. The first Europeans wandering through the area in the early 1500's encountered extensive park-like longleaf pine forests. These forests developed when fires occurred every 2-3 years. Some think that the Indians set fires to improve hunting and to make for easier travel. Others think that fires were at one time a common natural feature of the Grand Strand due to a drier climate. Regardless of the origin of historical fires, it is clear that fires are now less frequent than in the past. When forest fires do break out during dry spells in summer, the blazes can be intense and houses built near forests are in danger of being destroyed. Forest fires will likely become more and more of a problem in the Grand Strand as housing developments encroach on areas supporting dense stands of pines and shrubs.

The nearly constant wind off the Atlantic Ocean prunes trees and other vegetation.

Hurricanes and the torrential rains that accompany them, are facts of life in the Grand Strand. The storm surge erodes the beach and rearranges the distribution of sand along the beach. Even though it is well established that beaches move with the forces of nature, humans continue to build and rebuild on the beach. Maintenance of the Grand Strand beach often occurs by a process called renourishment. Here, sand is dredged from offshore sites, brought to the beach, and then deposited on the beach. Few tourists recognize the foreign sand under their feet. Further inland, hurricane impacts are expressed primarily as flooding in low areas. Many homes along the Waccamaw River were destroyed by Hurricane Floyd in 1999 and are not being rebuilt.

With hurricanes, fires, floods, and extensive wetland areas not suitable for building, it seems unlikely that human development of the Grand Strand would proceed very quickly. However, this is one of the fastest growing areas of the state primarily due to an unprecedented influx of permanent residents. These permanent residents are attracted by the climate, the beach, the services, and the general quality of life. These permanent residents are also demanding better protection of the natural features of the area. Stormwater management, water quality, green space, wetlands, rare species, and scenic vistas are all issues that must now be balanced with the forces that make new places for humans to live and play. Hopefully, visitors to the Grand Strand and permanent residents alike will find that this balance has been achieved in the future.

James Luken
Richard Moore

Animals of the
Grand Strand

American Alligator

Alligators bask on the bank.

Do they live here?

In case you were wondering, yes, the Grand Strand is home to the American alligator. This species ranges from the Florida Everglades to North Carolina. The coastal marshes, rivers, abandoned rice fields, and ponds of South Carolina are particularly well-suited for supporting healthy populations of alligators. Indeed, any body of fresh or brackish water along the Grand Strand should be considered as potential alligator habitat. In South Carolina alligators reach adult size (6 feet long) in about 5 years.

What do they do?

Alligators spend most of their time on exposed mud banks where they bask in the sun. This sluggish demeanor is somewhat deceptive because an alligator can move pretty quickly when it decides to eat something. Juvenile alligators eat fish, frogs, and insects. Adults will consume whatever they can catch and swallow. Alligators invading residential lakes or golf course ponds inevitably cause problems because tame ducks and pets begin disappearing. At that point the animal control people are called in for a removal.

What you won't see but should know.

Female alligators build nests of dead vegetation and then deposit their eggs inside the mound. As the mound begins to rot, heat is produced, incubating the eggs. Mound temperature determines the sex of hatchlings. Cool mounds produce more females; warm mounds produce more males. The alligators hatch in about 2 months and the babies remain together as a group for up to 3 years. Females aggressively protect the babies. If you see a baby alligator do not try to catch it.

Where can I see an alligator?

During the warm months, alligators can be observed cruising along the causeway at Huntington Beach State Park. However, many tourists drive this road and miss seeing the animals. Look for swimming gators with their heads protruding slightly above the water. Sometimes they look like floating debris. Do not fish for crabs or use live bait when alligators are in the area. An alligator entangled in a net is a real hazard. Boaters making the trip to Sandy Island and the Waccamaw National Wildlife Refuge will find many smaller alligators swimming in the creeks that feed the Waccamaw River. Bigger gators live in the Waccamaw River, but these individuals are secretive and are seldom observed.

See also: Huntington Beach State Park, rice field, Sandy Island, Waccamaw National Wildlife Refuge

Ark Clam

Our most common clam

Walk along any Grand Strand beach and chances are high that you will see large numbers of ark clam shells. They often accumulate in lines marking the reach of the last high tide. There are several species of ark clam that occur in our area, but the most common one is the incongruous ark. This clam has a shell with prominent ribs that extend from the bump and continue to the outer edge, sweeping to one side so that individual shells are not symmetrical. All species of ark clam have a line of small teeth where the two shells meet and form a hinge. These small teeth help to lock the two halves in place. Ark clams live partially buried in the sand or mud. They are filter feeders and may be the most important clam in shallow waters just off of the Grand Strand beach.

The blood of ark clams

Ark clams are interesting because of the presence of hemoglobin in their blood. This substance gives blood the red color and is the same molecule found in human blood. Hemoglobin carries oxygen and may explain why ark clams are able to live in some oxygen-poor bottom environments.

Ark holes

If you carefully examine the ark shells collected on the beach, most are covered with small holes on the surface or they have gaps at the shell edges. These holes and gaps are the work of various predatory snails. Specifically, moon snails, whelks, and oyster drills all prey on ark clams by drilling or rubbing openings in the shell. Note how many times the snails attempted to drill holes, but were not successful in completing the task. Consider also how many holes were completed. Apparently, an ark clam can tolerate a fair amount of predation before dieing.

See also: coquina, knobbed whelk, moon snail, oyster drill, ribbed mussel

Atlantic Croaker

Croaker characteristics

Pier fishermen along the Grand Strand probably catch more Atlantic croakers than any other fish species. The croaker, a member of the drum family, is named because of the grinding sound it makes when taken from the water. This sound is the result of vibrating muscles located near the swim bladder. The Atlantic croaker is a silver fish with diagonal bars along the side. It has extremely short barbels under the lower jaw that are often worn away, and when caught, will flare out its gill covers. The gill covers have sharp edges and can cause deep cuts. Croakers are found in near shore areas and estuaries during spring, summer, and fall.

Getting more croakers

The reproduction cycle of the Atlantic croaker is similar to the spot. Spawning occurs in near shore waters during late fall, but big female croakers with eggs have been captured far out to sea. Larval croakers are carried into the estuaries where they feed and grow until the summer of the next year. Once they reach a critical size, juvenile croakers then migrate back out to sea and take up residence in near shore waters or deep channels. Most croakers caught from Grand Strand piers are less then 12 inches long. It may take 4 years or longer for a croaker to get bigger than 12 inches.

Catching croakers

The Atlantic croaker is a bottom feeder. At the right time, usually an incoming tide, light tackle rigged with a 1-ounce sinker and tandem hooks will produce multiple catches. Small hooks (1/0 or narrower) are necessary; good baits include shrimp, squid, or bloodworms. Croakers are sold in seafood shops and fishermen often eat the ones that they catch. The fish is best filleted and then fried. Although catch limits for Atlantic croaker do not exist in South Carolina, it is prudent to keep only what you can quickly consume.

Photo by Don Millus

Catching croaker is fun for all ages.

See also: pinfish, red drum, spot, seatrout,

9

Menhaden school

Menhaden are migratory schooling fish in the herring family. They are recognized by green/brown coloration across the top, a forked tail, a spot just behind the gill cover, and a series of smaller spots along the mid section of the body. Visitors to the Grand Strand will likely experience menhaden during fall when large schools migrate south along the beach. Individual fish can get up to 1 foot long, but 6 inches is a more common size. Peak menhaden spawning occurs off the coast in late fall and winter and then fish begin moving northward in spring. Spawning may also occur during migration. Menhaden larvae move into estuaries where they grow to juvenile size. The juveniles eventually leave the estuaries and take up the migratory life.

Signs of feeding

As large schools of menhaden move through the Grand Strand region, many species of fish prey on them. Bluefish, seatrout, red drum, and others come into the schools and feed aggressively. When the menhaden are driven to the surface, gulls and terns also take advantage of the opportunity. It is not uncommon to see hundreds of gulls circling a school of menhaden in anticipation of a bluefish attack. Fisherman also follow the gulls if they are searching for bait and bait-eaters.

The ocean's Filter Feeder

Menhaden feed on microscopic plankton. They do this by swimming through the water and filtering food with specialized gill rakers. Individual fish can filter up to 7 gallons of water every minute. It is thought that menhaden in large schools can filter so much material that water clarity actually improves. This in turn lets more light down into the water and stimulates plant growth. Menhaden may also crop down excessive algal blooms, thereby removing nutrients from the water. Blooms of toxic algae have been implicated in fish kills, and some think that over harvest of menhaden might contribute to this. Declining menhaden stocks in the northeast are associated with malnutrition and poor health of striped bass.

So many uses

Indians and the early colonists recognized the value of menhaden as fertilizer. Indeed, the first large menhaden fishery developed in the northeast in an effort to supply farmers with fish. In the late 1800's menhaden were captured for their oil and then in the early 1900's menhaden were caught and processed into livestock feed. Most recently, with the help of spotter airplanes and large purse seine nets, menhaden are caught, processed into fish meal, or used to produce various edible oils that might provide health benefits to people. Intensive use of menhaden stocks is controversial since the species serves as a vital link between microscopic plankton and larger predatory fish.

Large schools of menhaden support commercial fisheries.

See also: bluefish, red drum, seatrout

Barnacle

Barnacles grow on piers and pilings near the tidal line.

Barnacle biology

Although they are related to crabs and shrimp, barnacles are so highly modified for attachment to hard substrates that this relationship is not apparent. Barnacles are backwards in many ways. The antennae are used for attachment to hard surfaces. The six pairs of legs are not for movement but instead comprise a net-like structure that is extended and repeatedly swept through the water in efforts to filter out small particles of food. The body of the barnacle is surrounded by pairs of hard plates. The outer plates are fixed to the substrate, but the inner plates move so that barnacles can cover up during periods of stress. All barnacles live in marine environments. Some occur in deep waters, but the familiar acorn barnacles we see along the Grand Strand grow on rocks, pilings, clams, loggerhead sea turtles, and the bottoms of boats.

Getting more barnacles

Barnacles engage is some very interesting sexual antics. Adults are not mobile, but males and females exist close to each other on the substrate. Getting sperm to nearby females is done with a relatively long male reproductive organ or penis. The proportion of penis length to body length is larger than for any other animal! Females hold the fertilized eggs until they hatch. Larvae are mobile and are moved with the water currents, eventually settling on hard substrates and remaining attached to that one spot for the rest of their lives.

Barnacles on the rocks

In the northeast where the intertidal zone is rocky rather than sandy, barnacles have been intensively studied in efforts to understand why different species occur in different intertidal zones. One species may dominate the high and relatively dry rocks; another species may dominate the low and relatively wet rocks. Apparently, the sorting of species is linked to differences in growth rates and abilities to tolerate the high temperatures of exposed rocks. Along the Grand Strand the best place to see barnacles growing in a range of exposure conditions is the jetty at Huntington Beach State Park. Time your visit for low tide and you will also see a variety of marine algae.

All fouled up

Barnacles can be a nuisance when they attach themselves to the bottoms of boats and to the lower parts of boat engines. Boats left in the water for long periods of time have to be periodically hauled out and scraped clean of the barnacles. Special paints have been developed in efforts to repel the larvae, but eventually any hard substrate left in sea water will get colonized.

See also: blue crab, ribbed mussel, seaweed, shrimp

Beaver

Beaver photos courtesy of Steve Smith

Once gone, now returned

Although beavers are now common in freshwater habitats along the Grand Strand, this was not always the case. Trapping and hunting in the late 1800's almost eliminated them from the entire state of South Carolina. However, a reintroduction program in the 1940's was very successful and now beavers occur in high numbers throughout the state.

The beaver as an engineer

Beavers have an irrepressible urge to build dams. They construct dams from tree trunks, sticks, and mud. The best evidence of beavers is the presence of blunt tree stumps that remain after the trunks were completely severed by gnawing. In the sluggish streams of coastal South Carolina, the dams create ponds and wetlands. Studies show that these beaver ponds in turn provide useful habitat for plants, reptiles, fish and birds. Indeed, beavers are known as ecological engineers because of their impacts on aquatic systems.

Beaver dam.

The beaver as a nuisance

Beavers are busy animals and they pursue their engineering activities regardless of human presence. Many houses along the Grand Strand are built near ponds. When beavers move in, landscape plants and sometimes even houses and fences get gnawed. Farmers are often perplexed to find flooded fields after beavers clogged drainage ditches and culverts. Wildlife specialists are kept very busy along the Grand Strand removing beavers and destroying the structures that they build.

Searching for beavers

Beavers are nocturnal. The best time to see beavers is at dusk when they emerge from their dens and begin searching for food. Sit quietly by a pond where there is evidence of recent beaver activity (gnawed trees) and you will likely be treated to a sight of North America's largest rodent.

Trees chewed by beavers

See also: American alligator, bowfin, freshwater wetland, yellow-bellied slider

Black Bear

Black Bears are becomming increasingly rare in coastal South Carolina.

Where are the bears?

Biologists estimate that about 250 black bears live in the coastal region stretching from Georgetown County in South Carolina to Brunswick County in North Carolina. Although bears are by nature very secretive, sightings are on the increase in the Grand Strand. Most commonly a golfer will glimpse a bear running across the fairway, or a homeowner will see one peering from the edge of the woods in the backyard. Many of these sightings occur in developments that border Lewis Ocean Bay Heritage Preserve. This preserve provides excellent bear habitat in the form of dense Carolina Bays. Although seeing a bear in the open is exciting, it indicates that humans are encroaching on bear habitat and that bears are being forced to move in the open as they forage for food.

Bear habits

Bears need both food and cover. A female bear will roam throughout a 10-square-mile area as she searches for food. Male bears need even larger areas. Critical bear habitat along the Grand Strand is provided by Carolina Bays. These elliptically-shaped depressions support nearly impenetrable thickets of shrubs and trees. Bears use these bays as rest areas, escape areas, feeding areas, and den areas. However, when food supplies are scarce, bears start to move and then they wander into dangerous areas. Bears along the Grand Strand face two direct threats: highway fatality and harassment by dogs.

A plan to connect Grand Strand bears

Wildlife biologists hope to eventually create a large bear sanctuary that will stretch from Lewis Ocean Bay Heritage Preserve to the Waccamaw National Wildlife Refuge. The plan includes underpasses for bears to cross busy highways as well as continuous corridors of forest that will allow easy and safe bear movements. Although the land parcels are not yet all under protection, this plan is the solution for ensuring long-term survival of Grand Strand bears.

Where can I see a bear?

Your best chance of seeing a bear is in Lewis Ocean Bay Heritage Preserve. Walk quietly along the gravel roads or along the edges of Carolina Bays. If you do see a bear, keep your distance and enjoy the moment.

See also: Lewis Ocean Bay Heritage Preserve, Waccamaw River Heritage Preserve, Waccamaw National Wildlife Refuge

Blue Crab

There are many ways to catch a crab.

The crab you catch and eat

Blue crabs are much pursued in the Grand Strand region because of their relatively large size and excellent flavor. Indeed, they are considered the only crab of any commercial importance. This is a swimming species that lives in estuaries and the ocean depending on the stage of development. They are recognized by the blue color and the presence of large claws. Males differ from females in the shape of the abdomen. A male has a long, inverted T-shaped abdomen. A female has an inverted V or U-shaped abdomen. Males are usually larger than females and may reach 8 inches from point-to-point.

What do they eat?

Blue crabs eat just about anything. Active predators, they will consume clams, fish, oysters, and snails. Indeed, research shows that they control the abundance of many bottom-dwelling organisms. They have the ability to sense oily tissues and thus are attracted to dead animals of all kinds.

Where do they go?

The migration of blue crabs is keyed to the stage of the life cycle and to the current water conditions. Mating occurs in rivers or estuaries but, after mating, females move to the ocean where spawning occurs. Females carrying masses of eggs are known as sponge crabs and are protected by law. Microscopic larvae are carried out to sea but are then washed back into the shallow water of the estuaries where the juveniles live. Once they get large enough to avoid predators, crabs may move once again into the ocean. During molts, crabs move into shallow waters to avoid predators.

Going crabbing

Blue crabs can be caught in warmer months by using a variety of techniques. They must be at least 5 inches from point to point. It is also a good idea to release females. Crab pots can be dropped in shallow waters, but these must be marked with floats. Most visitors purchase inexpensive drop nets and then use them from bridges or docks. Popular baits include chicken necks and fish heads. Crabs should be handled with tongs or heavy gloves to avoid getting pinched. Keep them dry and alive by placing in a cooler or bucket. Crabs are best when steamed for 20 minutes. Removal of the sweet tissue takes some practice, but it is well worth the trouble.

See also: fiddler crab, ghost crab, Huntington Beach State Park, salt marsh, periwinkle

Bluefish

Start here for fast action

Although bluefish get mixed reviews when it comes to their flavor, no one disputes the fact that this is a great sporting fish. Indeed, anglers visiting the Grand Strand who are a bit intimidated by the great variety of saltwater fish might start first by targeting this species. They are easy to catch. They fight like crazy. And they are readily available almost year round. However, if you typically fish for bream or bass and you think that your light tackle will work on bluefish, think again.

What do thy do?

Bluefish are migratory fish-eating machines. They move up the Atlantic coast in spring and then move down the coast in fall. Schools consist of similar-sized fish. Along the Grand Strand, larger blues (>5 lbs) can be caught offshore in spring as they migrate through the area. Smaller blues (usually 2-3 lbs and called snappers), can be caught in spring, summer and fall around inlets, in estuaries, and in the surf.

When bluefish feed

The spectacle of bluefish feeding at the surface will not be easily forgotten. Surface feeding begins in late summer and early fall when schools of baitfish congregate in shallow waters. Bluefish chase the baitfish and eventually force them to the surface where they leap for their lives. As they fall back into the water the sound is that of a short but intense cloud burst. Often Spanish mackerel, terns and gulls also feed in the same arena. At these times, the choice of lure is not important. However, you need at least 30 pound test monofilament or a wire leader. Be prepared to replace your lures often as the teeth of bluefish are sharp and efficient. Many bluefish are taken from piers and from the surf by the use of bottom rigs and cut bait. Actively feeding bluefish can also be taken on a fly rod, but again a wire tippet is required. Use pliers or a wire mesh glove to deal with hooked bluefish. When bluefish feed, surfers and swimmers are advised to go elsewhere.

Dealing with the catch

South Carolina law allows fishermen to keep 15 bluefish per day with no size restrictions. Such a generous limit should be placed in perspective. Bluefish stocks are on the decline in many parts of the Atlantic coast and thus fishermen should keep only what they plan to eat and then release the others. Some anglers "bleed" bluefish immediately after catching them. This can be done by cutting off the tail. Others immediately filet the fish and remove the dark-colored tissue. Keep the filets on ice as the flesh quickly begins to deteriorate. Bluefish have soft-textured tissue that makes a good stew. Alternatively, filets can be basted with Italian dressing and then baked or grilled.

See also: flounder, Myrtle Beach State park, pinfish, spots

Bottlenose Dolphin

The mammal, not the fish

The bottlenose dolphin, the most common marine mammal seen along the Grand Strand, gets its name from the short, broad snout that extends from the dome-shaped head. The jaws are filled with teeth and the upper jaw is shorter than the lower jaw. A well-defined, curved dorsal fin cuts through the water when bottlenose dolphins swim near the surface. (The dorsal fin takes on various unique markings that allow individual animals to be identified for research purposes.) The gray color of the body coupled with the dorsal fin often cause some people to assume sharks are present. However, bottlenose dolphins swim in groups (pods); sharks rarely show their dorsal fins in the relatively deep waters of the Grand Strand and do not usually swim in groups. A fish, called the dolphin, dorado, or Mahi Mahi, is pursued by offshore anglers.

Local dolphins

Bottlenose dolphins are widely distributed in coastal and offshore waters around the world. However, distinct populations have been identified in terms of migratory habits. Some bottlenose dolphins are year around residents in the near shore and estuarine waters of the Grand Strand. Other bottlenose dolphins are migratory, heading north along the coast in spring and then moving south in the fall. All Grand Strand bottlenose dolphins follow and harass schools of mullet and menhaden while these baitfish move along the coast. During summer, bottlenose dolphins are seen swimming far up the Waccamaw River in search of catfish. In fall and winter, bottlenose dolphins swim far up the tidal creeks in search of cold, sluggish fish. Sport fishermen are convinced that bottlenose dolphin feed excessively on spotted seatrout and red drum during winter. This controversial issue is currently under study.

Feeding

Veteran dolphin watchers along the Grand Strand can identify various feeding tactics. Often bottlenose dolphins swim in tight pods and then make short but sudden runs into schools of baitfish. They locate the prey by using sophisticated echolocation. Other times, they slap the water with their tails in an effort to herd baitfish. Most impressive is the strand feeding observed in some tidal creeks. Here, pods of bottlenose dolphins chase baitfish out of the water and onto the mud bank. The dolphins also come out of the water and snatch as many of the flopping fish as possible. When bottlenose dolphins are chasing bait, it is common for gulls and terns to also participate in the feeding frenzy.

Dolphin dangers

Bottlenose dolphins are curious creatures and are attracted to boats. They sometimes ride the wakes left by boats. Unfortunately, bottlenose dolphins also are attracted to commercial fishing operations where accidental entanglement in nets causes some mortality. Occasionally, bottlenose dolphins are struck by the propellers of power boats.

See also: bluefish, mullet, Atlantic menhaden, red drum, seatrout, spot

Bowfin

What is this thing on the end of my line?

Bass fishermen pulling their lures through the dark and sluggish waters of the Waccamaw River may encounter a formidable fish known as the bowfin or mudfish. This primitive species, the last of a line that lived more than 50 million years ago, is easily recognized by the smooth flat head, toothy mouth, rounded tail and the long dorsal fin. Bowfins have a swim bladder that functions as a lung. They gulp air at the surface and are thus superbly adapted for life in waters where oxygen levels are extremely low.

Bowfins are active predators and will consume just about anything that moves, including other bowfins. Individuals in the 4-6 lb range are very common in the Waccamaw River. However, the world record bowfin (21 pounds) was caught in Forest Lake, South Carolina, in 1980.

When bowfin strike

Grand Strand fishermen are split on the sporting qualities of bowfins. Serious bass fishermen consider bowfins as trash fish. To add insult to injury, bowfins, once hooked, will often destroy the lures they have attacked. However, a large cadre of fishermen on the Waccamaw River frequently pursue bowfins because they fight just like pike or muskies.

Bowfins are caught in the same types of habitats as largemouth bass. Try flipping plastic worms to beds of waterlilies and near wood. They also can be caught on live or cut bait. However, their serious teeth mean two things: use a wire leader or 30-lb monofilament and keep your fingers away from the mouth.

Can you eat a bowfin?

In some parts of the country bowfins are eaten. The flesh is soft and is best smoked or used in stews. If you catch bowfins from the Waccamaw River or for that matter any river in the Grand Strand area, do not eat them. As top predators their meat carries a high load of mercury that is unsafe at any level of consumption. However, bowfins do produce a shiny black roe known as "Cajun caviar," now being commercially produced in some parts of the country.

Why are bowfins important?

Bowfins are probably the most important predatory fish in the Waccamaw River. Biologists think that bowfins serve an important role in controlling the numbers of bream and sunfish. By removing many small fish from the populations, a few of the bream can reach larger sizes. Bowfin may also remove sick or diseased fish.

Where is the best place to catch bowfins?

The Waccamaw River from Peachtree Landing to the Savannah Bluff Landing is prime bowfin territory. This section of the river is strongly influenced by tides. On a rising tide fish will be more scattered among the bald cypress trees. On a falling tide, fish will be more concentrated in weed beds.

See also: bream, freshwater wetland, rice fields, Waccamaw National Wildlife Refuge

Bream

Redbreast sunfish get their names from their reddish orange bellies. *Bluegill or brim usually have large dark spots near the back of their dorsal fin.*

Redear or Shellcracker. *The pumpkinseed is usually a small, rounded sunfish, with wavy lines on its head and a red spot on the gill cover.*

A family of fish for family fishing

In South Carolina the term "bream" refers to a group of eight different sunfishes. All are relatively small and tend to be widely distributed in streams, rivers, lakes, and ponds. Fishing in fresh waters along the Grand Strand is likely to produce four of the eight: bluegill, pumpkinseed, redbreast sunfish, and redear sunfish. Bream fishing is perhaps the most popular type of fishing done by the locals. This is because bream can be caught from the bank and because populations are relatively high in comparison to bass and other more glamorous game fish.

Which is which?

The bluegill has a short black flap protruding from the operculum, a bronze belly, and vertical bars along the side. The redbreast sunfish has a reddish orange breast with a very long black flap protruding from the operculum. The redear sunfish, also known as the shellcracker, is widely stocked in ponds and grows to relatively large sizes. The black flap on the operculum (gill cover) has a red edge. Big redear sunfish have speckled sides. The smaller pumpkinseed also has red on its gill cover, but this is limited to a small spot rather than the entire edge. The pumpkinseed also has wavy green lines on its head below the eye.

Bream move in different directions

Although the various species of sunfish may look alike, they do differ in their spawning activities. All sunfish begin spawning activities when water temperatures reach 70 degrees F. Bluegill and redear sunfish build nests (depressions) in shallow, still waters. Sand and mud are preferred substrates. These species are more suited to life in ponds and sloughs. The redbreast sunfish builds nests associated with downed wood and it will spawn in the main channels of rivers. Invasion of the Waccamaw River by flathead catfish has affected populations of redbreast sunfish because spawning adults are susceptible to being eaten by the big cats. Sunfish feed on aquatic insects and other invertebrates, but the redear sunfish has special teeth that allow it to crush especially hard food items.

Bream tactics

Locals pursue bream with cane poles and crickets. The standard approach on the Waccamaw is to float slowly down the river while targeting downed wood, bald cypress trees, and small pockets in the bank. Just about any pond along the Grand Strand will yield plenty of bream action for children who are short on patience. However, as with other freshwater fish in the Waccamaw system, bream pick up mercury from the water and thus consumption should be limited.

See also: bald cypress, bowfin, largemouth bass, Waccamaw River Heritage Preserve

Broad-headed Skink 13

The male broadhead skink has a wide red head.

Female and juvenile skinks have lines down their backs. (inset)

A very large lizard

Your first encounter with a broad-headed skink can be memorable. These animals get up to a foot long, they have thick necks reminiscent of the dragons that patrol more tropical locations, and they are fast. Indeed, the broad-headed skink is one of our largest lizards. Most of the time they are olive or light tan but, during the breeding season, the heads on males take on a bright orange or red coloration. The myth is that broad-headed skinks are poisonous and thus some people refer to them as scorpions. Yes, they will bite repeatedly when handled but these animals rely on force rather than poison to catch prey.

Where do they live?

Broad-headed skinks naturally take to the trees where they prefer the holes and crevices of live oaks. Along the Grand Strand, broad-headed skinks live under decks and porches. While sitting quietly on a porch, you will often be startled to see a hefty broad-headed skink run out into the open, grab an insect snack, and then quickly retreat to the shade. Broad-headed skinks eat a large variety of insects and invertebrates and thus should be considered useful predators in the residential landscape.

Boys in battle

Male broad-headed skinks are prone to many interesting behaviors during the breeding season. Most of these behaviors are for one purpose: getting a mate. Size and coloration of the head carries a lot of weight in male-on-male competition. Thus, when two competing males meet on the battlefield, they compare heads in elaborate display rituals. If the fashion show does not resolve the issue of who is better, then a good wrestling match will often follow.

Smelling the air

Broad-headed skinks constantly sample the air by flicking their tongues. They have the ability to detect low levels of chemicals. In some instances this allows them to find and track prey. In other instances, chemical messages are used to transmit information about their fellow broad-headed skinks. Thus, tongue-flicking increases in frequency when two skinks meet.

See also: alligator, eastern cottonmouth, green anole, live oak

19

Brown Pelican

14

Brown Pelicans are commonly seen along the Grand Strand.   Pelican nest at Cape Romain Nationanl Wildlife Refuge.

What is it?

The brown pelican is a large bird that visitors to the Grand Strand will commonly see flying low along the beach. Up close the brown pelican is easy to recognize because of the long brown bill equipped with a pouch. In flight, adult birds are marked by the white patch on the head and neck. This is the largest bird on the beach with a 6-7 foot wingspan. Brown pelicans shun freshwater and can be found along the coasts of the Atlantic Ocean, the Gulf of Mexico, and the Pacific Ocean. They rarely venture far out to sea.

Peering at pelicans

Brown pelicans are unique both when flying and when feeding. They fly with a characteristic flap-and-glide pattern that often takes them in anything but a straight line. Perhaps such a flight path helps in their constant search for fish such as menhaden, pinfish, and mullet. When schools of fish are sighted, a brown pelican will suddenly dive into the water. The dive appears awkward, characterized by open wings and open bill, but it must be effective because brown pelicans often emerge from the water with a pouch full of fish.

What about the pouch?

The pouch under the bill has dual functions. First, it serves as a type of bag for gathering fish. As brown pelicans emerge from the water after a dive, water in the pouch is pushed out the corners of the bill. Fish are then swallowed and temporarily stored in the gullet (not the pouch). Brown pelicans also expose the pouch to the wind and thereby achieve a cooling effect. The pouch, serving as a heat exchanger, may explain why brown pelicans can tolerate the heat of summer that drives other animals into the shade.

Brown pelicans back from the brink

Brown pelicans numbering in the thousands have persisted in coastal regions of South Carolina. However, in other states such as Louisiana and Mississippi, populations declined dramatically during the late 1950's. This reduction was eventually traced to the toxic effects of the pesticide DDT. Declines were so severe that the brown pelican was listed as an endangered species in 1970. The elimination of widespread DDT use has allowed many brown pelican populations to recover. Other current threats to brown pelicans include human disturbance of nesting colonies and entanglement in fishing equipment.

A tendency to tame

Most fishing piers and docks along the Grand Strand have at least one brown pelican that has abandoned the wild life in favor of handouts from fishermen. These birds sit quietly and patiently waiting for the bite to begin. As the reels start cranking the pelicans (as well as people) move to better positions so that the catch can be inspected. Although, some might argue that a tame brown pelican is a sad sight, the birds do provide encouragement and companionship for fishermen during those long periods when the fish aren't biting.

See also: double-crested cormorant, great blue heron, great egret, gull

Canada Goose

Our golf course goose

Honking of the Canada goose is a common sound around parks, subdivisions, and golf courses of the Grand Strand. Our resident geese are large (up to 40 inches) and are typically observed as pairs or as small flocks. They have a gray body, black neck and a distinctive white throat patch. Grand Strand Canada geese are non-migratory, living and reproducing in the Grand Strand. They are larger than other subspecies of Canada goose, which are migratory.

Getting more geese

Around the Grand Strand, Canada geese begin their nesting activities in late winter. Males and females mate for life and may use the same nest site year after year. Nests are usually constructed on small peninsulas or islands of subdivision or golf course ponds. Nests are made of grass or emergent plants and once eggs are laid, birds actively defend the nest from all intruders. Many Grand Strand golfers have been chased away from the edge of a pond by hissing Canada geese. In about 1 month the eggs hatch and the young soon begin looking for food.

Taking up residence

Prior to the 1950's most of the Canada geese observed in South Carolina were migratory birds. They wintered here but flew to the far north of Canada to reproduce. By the 1980's this population of geese had dwindled due a variety of factors. Most importantly, greater availability of food and habitat in northern states tended to short-stop the geese during their travels. Some of these geese stopped migrating completely and became permanent northern residents. When these Yankee birds grew in numbers, some were trapped and introduced to South Carolina. Descendents of these non-migratory geese are the ones we likely see now around the Grand Strand.

Goose problems

Canada geese are grazers that feed on grass in open areas such as golf courses, cattle pastures, and municipal parks. Indeed, Grand Strand geese typically move their families to golf courses as soon as the young can make the trip. However, their droppings and feeding activities create problems for golf course managers. Scare guns and chemical repellants have been used to move the geese to other areas. But with nearly 100 golf courses available for use along the Grand Strand, it is likely that the geese simply leave one golf course and then take up residence in another.

See also: double-crested cormorant, great blue heron, wood duck

Coquina Clam

The small coquina clam lives in the beach just at the tide's edge.

The clam at your feet

One of the few organisms that live in the surf zone of the beach is the small coquina clam. Because coquina clams can quickly burrow in constantly shifting sand, they are well-suited to this stressful environment. They occur by the thousands and can be recognized by the triangular shape and great variety of colors. Coquina clams can be found by simply digging with your feet where the waves wash over the sand. These small clams will be exposed, but not for long. Be quick with your hands if want to examine them closer.

Coquina clams on the move

Coquina clams remain in the swash zone of the beach. As tides rise and fall this swash zone moves. Coquina clams ride the waves up the beach with a rising tide. They also ride the waves down the beach with a falling tide. When not riding the waves, coquina clams use a small siphon to suck in water, filtering particles of food out of the water and then expelling the water through a different siphon. The surf zone is rich in food particles thus allowing many thousands of coquina clams to live and reproduce. Coquina clams that get washed into deeper waters may be eaten by moon snails.

Coquina clam shells as a building material

The word "coquina" also refers to a type of sedimentary rock that consists of sand and coquina shells. This rock formed when deposits of coquina shells were exposed by falling sea levels. In the late 1600's and 1700's, the Spanish and the British mined this material and used it to build forts. The shells are excellent for absorbing the impacts of cannon balls. Most recently, coquina is mined, ground, and then used as a road-building material.

Coquina come in many colors and patterns.

See also: hard clam, moon snail, oyster, oyster drill, ribbed mussel

Double-Crested Cormorant

Cormorant flying over Murrells Inlet.   *Double-crested cormorants are common winter birds along the Grand Strand. (inset)*

What is it?

The double-crested cormorant is a dark, fish-eating, water bird found in or near all aquatic habitats of the Grand Strand. It is easy to identify based on large size, a hooked bill, forked tail, and the orange throat patch. When on the move, double-crested cormorants fly in small groups with necks crooked. They awkwardly land in perch sites. While swimming, double-crested cormorants sit low in the water, but diving for fish is often preceded by a short leap out of the water. This species has recently shown some impressive population gains all across the country.

The wing pose

Double-crested cormorants have a strange tendency to perch in trees with their wings outstretched. This behavior usually occurs immediately after the birds emerge from the water. Scientists originally thought that this was simply a way of drying out the feathers after a swim. However, the behavior may also serve to signal others in the group that a recent fishing trip was successful.

Fish beware

Of the many fish-eating birds found along the Grand Strand, the double-crested cormorant is perhaps the most accomplished. It dives to great depths and can actually out swim most fish. Tame cormorants are used in some Asian countries to commercially catch fish. Sport fishermen and commercial fish farmers have recently raised concern about increasing populations of double-crested cormorants. Studies show that the birds do not necessarily prey on the same species pursued by sport fishermen. However, fish farms, particularly catfish ponds, are vulnerable to a flock of cormorants. Efforts are underway in some southern states to reduce cormorant populations.

On the increase

Several factors have been linked to population increases of double-crested cormorants. Banning of DDT improved reproductive success as did protection of the birds under the Migratory Bird Treaty Act. Creation of reservoirs that support large schools of baitfish may also be contributing.

See also: brown pelican, great blue heron, great egret

Eastern Cottonmouth 18

The eastern cottonmouth is common near freshwater habitats of the Grand Strand.

One of several poisonous snakes

Within the Grand Strand region, the eastern cottonmouth or water moccasin is perhaps the most frequently encountered poisonous snake. It is common because of the large areas of small creeks, marshes, swamps, and ditches. Furthermore, cottonmouths can be active year around in these habitats. Identification of this species is difficult because of the wide range of colors and patterns. Indeed, the harmless brown water snake is often mistaken for the cottonmouth. However, if you find a dark, coiled snake that displays an open, white mouth, then you likely have a cottonmouth. This characteristic stance is a defensive posture.

What does it do?

A cottonmouth feeds at night and basks in the sun during the day. It will eat just about anything that is of the appropriate size. The potent venom injected via fangs is used to kill live prey, but the snake will also eat dead animals. These snakes function as top predators in aquatic systems and thus serve an important role in the maintenance of prey populations. Cottonmouths themselves are eaten by owls, turtles, and alligators.

Cottonmouth myths

The cottonmouth has a bad reputation. Some think that it is aggressive and prone to attacks on people. However, research conducted at the Savannah River Ecology Laboratory in South Carolina demonstrated that cottonmouths typically bite humans only when provoked or occasionally when stepped on. Biting with injection of venom is apparently reserved for prey capture.

The snake gets it name from the color of its mouth. The white lips are even visible when the mo is closed. But the white mouth shows best when the snake opens it mouth to threaten or strike.

Observe and enjoy

Treat all snakes with respect. When walking near water, be particularly careful near places where cottonmouths find both sun and a place to hide (e.g., hollow stumps or logs). Observing a cottonmouth from a distance can be exciting and rewarding. The observation period can also be long since cottonmouths do not flee when they encounter people!

See also: American alligator, green anole, Waccamaw National Wildlife Refuge, yellow-bellied slider

Fiddler Crab

The male fiddler crab uses his one larger claw as a display.   *Fiddler crab holes are most commonly found in muddy soils. (inset)*

Easy to see but as a group they flee

Visitors walking into Grand Strand salt marshes at low tide will find themselves herding large numbers of small crabs. (The herding behavior is actually a defense aimed at confusing predators.) These are fiddler crabs so named because the males have one claw that is much larger than the other. This large claw somewhat resembles a fiddle. A square yard of marsh may have up to 200 crabs and in the Grand Strand region there may be at least three different species. The different species have different preferences for substrates and salinity.

What about that giant claw?

Research suggests that the males use their giant claw for a variety of purposes, most of which are related to mating. Males wave the claw in the air to attract females. They also use it to ward off other males. And, when they have attracted a female to the mating burrow, they use it to bang on the sides of the burrow. The ability to make a good banging sound is apparently important in the eyes of the female. Interestingly, the giant claw is not so useful for feeding and thus the males have to work harder than females to get proper nutrition.

What do they eat?

Fiddler crabs, known as deposit feeders, comb through the soil and ingest small particles of dead plants and animals. When finished feeding they leave small balls of sediment on the soil surface. Fiddler crabs are themselves eaten by blue crabs and many different marsh birds.

Where do they go?

When not feeding, fiddler crabs excavate burrows that go down about 20 inches. The burrows and the working of sediment during construction of burrows have important effects in the salt marsh. Specifically, the burrows allow better drainage, they increase oxygen in the soil and may even lead to enhanced growth of smooth cordgrass. During winter, fiddler crabs retreat to their burrows, plug up the entrance with a ball of mud, and then live in small pockets of air. At this time they may suck water from the soil.

See also: blue crab, ghost crab, smooth cordgrass, salt marsh periwinkle

Finger Sponge

Sponges in many shapes and colors commonly wash up on Grand Strand beaches after storms.

Sponge facts

Sponges are simple invertebrates that live attached to the substrate. They come in a variety of shapes and colors. Because sponges cannot move, they must bring in their food. They do this with specialized cells that pump water through a system of pores and canals. Small particles of food are then trapped inside the sponge. The flow of water through sponges also brings in oxygen and removes carbon dioxide.

Sponges on the beach

Beachcombers along the Grand Strand commonly find stranded individuals of the finger sponge. When bounced onto the beach, this species is tan or brown, but it will turn white in the sun. It has branched, fingerlike projections and a well-defined stalk at the base. When squeezed, the finger sponge feels like ... sponge.

Action on the bottom

The ocean bottom along the Grand Strand is mostly flat and sandy. However, there are patches of hard bottom here and there. These patches, known as "active bottom," allow establishment of a wide variety of attached animals like barnacles, sponges and corals. Indeed, the finger sponge is one of the most important animals on these active bottoms. Finger sponges found on the beach have likely been dislodged by winds, waves, or trawlers.

Sponge hotels

Finger sponges provide habitat and food for other animals. Polychaete worms live in the pores and channels of the finger sponge. They also likely dine on food particles brought into the sponge. Small fish use the three-dimensional structure of the finger sponge as habitat. The locations of active bottom are well known to local fishermen as these areas also attract many different types of game fish.

See also: barnacle, jellyfish, polychaete worm, seatrout

Flathead Catfish

Photo courtesy of Fritz Rohde, NCDNR

This juvenile flathead catfish could grow to weigh over thirty pounds.

A new fish in the neighborhood

The flathead catfish, a relatively new addition to the Waccamaw River, is native to the Mississippi River system. After it was introduced in the Pee Dee River during the 1960's it eventually found its way up into the Waccamaw. Flatheads, like other catfish, have well-developed whiskers that are used for locating prey. The top and sides of the body are mottled brown. The head is wide and flat, and the lower jaw extends beyond the upper jaw. Flathead catfish will grow to 50 lbs although fish in the 5 –6 lb range are the norm in the Waccamaw River.

Flathead habits

In contrast to many catfish that scavenge along the bottom, the flathead is an active predator. It feeds primarily on crayfish and fish. Flatheads prefer waterways that offer deep pools with cover. At night, they move out of the deep pools and hunt for prey in emergent and floating vegetation. The Waccamaw River is ideal for flatheads due to the presence of deep pools littered with sunken wood and large expanses of floating vegetation.

Flathead problems

Although the appearance of big flathead catfish in the Waccamaw River might at first seem innocuous, there is strong concern about how this big predator might affect populations of other fishes. In many rivers of the southeast, as flathead catfish expand in importance, populations of redbreast sunfish begin to decline. It is assumed that redbreast sunfish are relatively more vulnerable to the flatheads than are other species of sunfish. There is also the possibility that flatheads will move into brackish areas of the lower river where interactions with marine fishes could occur. The Waccamaw River supports a rich assemblage of native fishes and only time will tell how the flathead catfish changes this situation.

Catching cats

Catfish hunters on the Waccamaw focus their efforts in deep pools adjacent to weed beds. They fish at night with live bait. Although bluegill are preferred, other fish such as minnows will work as long as they are lively. Barrel weights above a short leader allow the bait to move in a small area while avoiding snags. Because flatheads get big and because the river bottom is littered with wood, strong line and heavy tackle are recommended. Flathead catfish should not be eaten because of mercury accumulation in the tissues.

See also: bowfin, bream, largemouth bass, Waccamaw National Wildlife Refuge, Waccamaw River Heritage Preserve

Flies

Horse flies are large, biting flies.

Deer flies and horse flies

Venture into a Grand Strand salt marsh or wetland during summer and chances are high that you will be attacked by large biting flies. These come in many sizes and colors but all of them have relatively large heads and eyes. Deer flies, about the size of house flies, typically have color patterns on the wings. Horse flies are larger than house flies and typically lack color patterns on the wings. The greenhead fly is a horse fly often found near beaches or salt marshes. These flies are a nuisance for people, horses, deer and other large vertebrates because the females feed on blood. The bite is painful, and the fly saliva includes an anticoagulant that assures that bleeding is profuse.

Getting more flies

Deer flies and horse flies lay their eggs on plant leaves that protrude above standing water or wet soil. The eggs hatch and the larvae take up residence in the mud where they develop and grow. Eventually, the larvae develop into pupae and then soon after, the adults emerge. The association of larvae with wet ground explains why marshes and wetlands are fly territories.

Out for blood

Deer flies and horse flies find victims primarily through sight. They wait at the edges of forests or near shrubs and perceive movement. Studies suggest that dark-colored objects are more easily spotted. The best time and condition for a fly attack is in the morning on a sunny day when there is little or no wind. Attacks consist of flies buzzing around the head or legs. Bites can occur almost immediately after a fly manages to land on skin.

Fly Problems

When livestock are attacked by many horse flies, blood loss can be substantial. Furthermore, these flies are known to transmit a variety of diseases. Some people have allergic reactions to fly saliva, leading to large sores at the site of the bite and more serious symptoms. There are few successful control methods for deer flies and horse flies. Some wading birds consume adult flies, but it is doubtful if this is an important control mechanism.

See also: great blue heron, great egret, mosquito, tick

Ghost Crab

Ghost crabs are sometimes seen in the daytime.

What do they look like?

Ghost crabs are true beach crabs that are often seen scurrying toward their burrows. They are recognized by their relatively large size (up to 2 inches wide), beige coloration, dark periscope eyes, and fast (up to 10 mph) speed. When in motion---which is most of the time---they are agile and can move quickly in all directions.

A day in their life

Ghost crabs excavate burrows above the high tide line. Larger crabs and thus larger burrows are found farthest from the water. Burrows slope downward and end in a chamber. During the heat of the day ghost crabs spend their time either resting or maintaining the burrow. At night, they emerge to search for food. Scavengers and predators, ghost crabs eat clams, other crabs, insects, seeds, and will even prey on baby turtles and turtle eggs. Larger animals washed up on the beach such as jellyfish and sharks will be picked to pieces by ghost crabs. Ghost crabs also consume food left by tourists. Periods of active feeding are punctuated by short trips to the surf where both water and oxygen are replenished. Females deposit eggs in the water during spring. The larvae initially live in the surf but eventually begin burrowing and working their way up the beach.

Sitting out winter

As air temperatures in fall turn cold and water temperatures drop, ghost crabs retire to their burrows, close up the openings, and wait for spring to come. At these times, they get water by sucking it from the surfaces of sand grains. This unique adaptation allows them to sit in the burrow for up to 6 months.

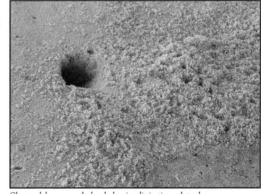

Chasing crabs

Children and adults first encountering a ghost crab will be faced with the irresistible urge to chase it. This is futile unless all burrow openings are blocked. It is also not recommended *Ghost crab burrow on the beach showing distinctive crab tracks.* as ghost crabs chased in the mid-day sun lose water rapidly and can eventually become dehydrated. It is perhaps more entertaining to follow crabs into their burrows and listen carefully for their threatening sounds.

See also: blue crab, fiddler crab, Huntington Beach State Park, sand dune

Great Blue Heron

Great blue herons are the largest wading bird commonly seen on the Grand Strand

What is it?

The great blue heron is a long-legged wading bird. With a height of 4 feet and a wingspan approaching 7 feet this is one of North America's largest birds. An adult great blue heron is grey-blue with white feathers around the head and neck and a black stripe above the eye. It has a spear-like bill that is used for killing prey. When at rest, the bird's long neck is bent upon itself so that the head seems to rest on the back. However, when the great blue heron is hunting, the neck is fully extended.

Where can I find it?

This heron is widely distributed in North America and Canada. Along the Grand Strand it is commonly seen at the edges of freshwater ponds and rivers, in drainage ditches, rice fields, and occasionally in shallow brackish waters. The best time to see a great blue heron hunting is at dawn or at dusk.

What does it eat?

The primary food of the great blue heron is fish. A solitary bird will stand motionless for long periods in shallow water waiting for the right opportunity to strike. Small bream are the preferred food, but fish as large as 12 inches can be speared and swallowed. The great blue heron will also eat frogs, turtles, snakes, crayfish, lizards and just about anything else that gets within reach of its bill. In rice fields, rats and mice are often stranded by rising waters. At these times, many of the rodents become food for the great blue heron.

The rookeries

South Carolina is home to several thousand breeding pairs of great blue herons. In late winter the birds congregate in well-defined areas known as rookeries where mating and nesting occur. Large and important rookeries with up to 800 nests are found near Lake Marion and Lake Moultrie in South Carolina. Smaller rookeries occur in swamps and near rivers of the coastal plain. Nests are often built in bald cypress or other tall trees. The male brings sticks for the nest and the female constructs the nest. Protection of rookeries from human disturbance is critical for long-term success of this species in South Carolina.

What's that sound?

Many visitors to the Grant Strand will hear at night a strange squawk. Most likely this is a great blue heron that has taken flight or has suddenly been disturbed by other night predators. Take some time to explore the area around your motel or condominium. You might see the animal that disturbed your sleep.

See also: freshwater wetland, Huntington Beach State Park, rice field, storm water detention pond

Great Egret

The Great Egret, also sometimes known as the common egret or American egret, is the largest white wading bird on the South Carolina coast.

The Snowy Egret looks rather like a miniature Great Egret, but differs in having a dark bill and yellow feet that are often visible even in muddy waters.

An outstanding egret

The great egret is one of the Grand Strand's largest wading birds. It is an all- white, heron-like bird that gets up to 3 feet tall. It has a long, yellow spear-shaped bill and black legs and feet. In late winter and spring, the great egret will show breeding plumage consisting of white ragged feathers hanging from the back and extending past the tail. Great egrets are commonly observed around the Grand Strand wading in salt marshes at the edges of creeks, ponds, and rice fields. Along the Grand Strand, great egrets are year-round residents. Another egret, the snowy egret, occurs along the Grand Strand. It is smaller and has a black bill, black legs, and yellow feet.

Egret feeding

The great egret wades slowly but deliberately in shallow water stalking fish, frogs, snakes, and crabs. A captured prey item too large for an easy gulp may be dropped and manipulated until it fits easily into the bird's mouth. Great egrets are often found feeding with flocks of white ibis. Some think that the egrets are picking off food items stirred off the bottom by the prodding of ibis bills.

Getting more egrets

Great egrets reproduce in groups called rookeries. The nests, made of sticks, are located in tall shrubs or trees. A large and very important rookery for great egrets occurs in the Washo Reserve, a bald cypress swamp located just south of the Santee River in South Carolina.

Hunted for the plumes

By the early 1900's great egrets were nearly hunted to extinction in North America. Market hunting was fueled by the craze for feathers, which were subsequently woven into fancy hats and other articles of clothing. The great egret was pursued primarily for the breeding plumes that brought as much as $80 an ounce. The decimation of many wading bird populations at this time led to the formation of the Audubon Society; the great egret served as an important symbol to publicize the need for better conservation practices. When market hunting ended, great egret populations recovered.

See also: great blue heron, osprey, white ibis

Green Anole

Commonly known as "chameleons" because of their ability to change color, the green anole is a member of same group of lizards as the iguana.

Male anoles display their red throats to attract females and warn other males away from their territories.   Anoles are common in gardens as well as forest habitats.

A changeable lizard

Although the Grand Strand region is home to many types of reptiles, the green anole is perhaps the one most commonly observed by visitors. This lizard is comfortable living in the tame but complex landscaped environments surrounding many of the resorts and residential areas. It is often observed scurrying across sidewalks or basking on the sides of buildings or fences. When cold or stressed, green anoles are dull brown. When warm, when attracting mates, or when fending off other lizards the green anole is bright green. This ability to change color prompts some to mistakenly call this species a chameleon. However, true chameleons change color to blend with the surroundings and the green anole appears to change colors for other reasons.

What's that red thing?

Male green anoles have a red, dime-sized flap of cartilage that can be displayed for attracting females or when the animal is defending a group of females. While involved in these manly activities, the lizards may also exhibit head bobbing. Apparently, the ability to put on a good show is the sign of a lizard in good shape and thus also a lizard suitable for mating--at least in the eyes of female lizards. Individual males may guard as many as six females!

Biological control of insects

Green anoles feast on insects, spiders, pill bugs and other invertebrates. When living in the exterior cracks and crevices of houses or in landscape shrubs, they no doubt provide some level of critter control. Thus green anoles should be encouraged and protected from cats and from harassment by small children.

Watching the show

Green anole watching can be great fun for children particularly during spring and fall. Males will often chase each other and do battle while females sit passively. Both males and females on cool days will move constantly in order to maximize their exposure to the sun. Insects entering the hunting space of a green anole are quickly gobbled, but swallowing can involve a bit more time and effort.

See also: broad-headed skink, eastern cottonmouth, yellow-bellied slider

Gull

The herring gull is the largest of the three common gulls. It is found on the Grand Strand mainly in the wintertime. Young birds are primarily brown colored. (left)
Laughing gulls are the common summer gull. Adults lose their black heads and red bills during the wintertime. (top right)
The ring-bill gulls gets its name from the ring around the tip of its bill. Ring-bill gulls are most common in the winter. (bottom right)

Gulls of the Grand Strand

Sun, sand, and surf do not make a complete beach experience unless gulls are somehow woven into the picture. Indeed, gulls are ubiquitous along the Grand Strand and they are the most common shore birds. Three gull species make up the majority of gull sightings: the herring gull, the ring-gilled gull, and the laughing gull. The herring gull is a large bird with a white body and gray across the tops of the winds. Its bill is yellow and there is no black band. The ring-billed gull is similar to the herring gull but it is smaller and the bill has a distinct black band near the tip. Both species are year around residents of the Grand Strand, although in some parts of the country gulls migrate north in spring to reproduce. The laughing gull is a summer resident of the Grand Strand. At this time it has a black head.

Gull babies

Gulls are colonial nesters. In South Carolina, nesting colonies are found on islands or on sand bars. The birds build their nests on the ground and typically lay three eggs. Gulls are noted for the color changes that occur with successive molts. Young-of-the-year gulls are gray or brown. These youngsters are often seen mixed with the adults.

Taking the opportunity to eat

Gulls are opportunistic feeders. They sense an abundant food source, and this information is quickly communicated to other members of the flock. Many visitors to the Grand Strand have tested this by offering food to a solitary gull. The solitary gull turns into hundreds of gulls and inevitably the generous tourist is the recipient of some randomly dropped gull poop. Most resorts along the beach do not allow the feeding of gulls for the simple reason that large flocks lead to large messes.

Scavengers of the parking lots

In summer and fall, gulls remain faithful to the sea where they find an abundance of fish in the water, crabs and clams in the salt marshes, and many types of food items deposited on the beaches. Most importantly they follow behind shrimp trawlers and commercial fishermen and eat whatever is discarded. However, in the depths of Grand Strand winters, gulls move inland in search of food. They congregate near the parking lots of large shopping centers where they find food dropped by shoppers. They gather in construction sites where earthworms can be plucked from the soil. In some parts of the country, they frequent the garbage dumps; this source of food has been linked to large population increases.

See also: brown pelican, hard clam, double-crested cormorant, fiddler crab, jellyfish

Hard Clam

Hard clamology

The hard clam, also known as the quahog, is the Grand Strand's commercially important clam. It is found buried in areas with muddy or sandy bottoms. Shell fragments of long-dead hard clams are also found on the beach. This species has a roundish, thick, heavy shell that ranges in color from brown to gray. There are concentric rings on the shell, and the inside leading edge has small indentations. Seafood stores sell hard clams graded and named by size. The smallest ones are called littlenecks; medium size hard clams are called cherrystones; and large hard clams are called chowders.

Ins and outs of clam feeding

Hard clams are filter feeders. They have two short tubes called siphons that extend from the shell. One siphon pulls water into the clam; the other siphon releases the water back into the ocean. As water moves into the clam body, algae and other small food items are filtered and trapped on the gills. The food eventually moves into the mouth of the hard clam. Blooms of toxic algae can render hard clams inedible. Likewise, bacteria associated with sewage can contaminate the bodies of hard clams.

Raising more clams

Individual hard clams may live up to 40 years, but they are able to reproduce after 2 years. Growth is relatively rapid in areas with constant, high salinity and warm water temperatures. Warm water temperatures stimulate female hard clams to release eggs into the water; males also release sperm. Fertilized eggs develop into mobile larvae, which eventually settle on the bottom and develop into clams. As with oysters, the presence of hard clams on the bottom attracts the settling of hard clam larvae. Thus, hard clams are found in dense patches. The hard clam is readily raised under controlled conditions; aquaculture of hard clams is a thriving industry in parts of the US.

Wampum from hard clam

Hard clams played an important role in the lives of coastal Indians. Indeed, the name "quahog" is an Algonquin name. The shell of the hard clam was used to make small purple beads called "wampum" that served as a form of valuable currency. Prior to contact with Europeans, wampum assumed value because of the inherent difficulty of cutting and drilling shell. After contact with Europeans and the introduction of metal tools, wampum was widely manufactured and for a short time it served as a standard form of trade currency. With time, however, metal coins supplanted wampum, and the shell beads took on more symbolic roles.

Seed clams growing in an aquaculture operation.

See also: knobbed whelk, lettered olive, moon snail, oyster, oyster drill, ribbed mussel, salt marsh periwinkle

Horseshoe Crab

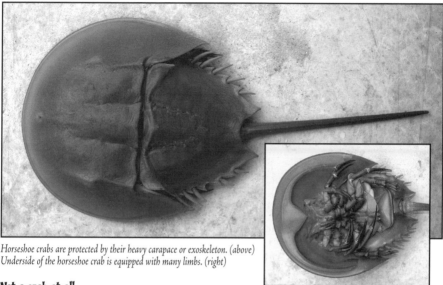

Horseshoe crabs are protected by their heavy carapace or exoskeleton. (above)
Underside of the horseshoe crab is equipped with many limbs. (right)

Not a crab at all

Horseshoe crabs or the empty shells of horseshoe crabs are sometimes found on Grand Strand beaches. These animals, although appearing mean and dangerous are quite harmless and are not at all like crabs. They are more closely related to spiders. This relationship is indicated by the seven pairs of legs and the presence of a pair of appendages near the mouth used for handling food. Horseshoe crabs have two pairs of eyes. The mean facial expression of horseshoe crabs comes from the shape and orientation of the pair of eyes located about halfway down the shell.

What do they do?

Horseshoe crabs live in estuaries and in the open ocean. They crawl along the bottom feeding on worms, clams, and dead animals. In spring, horseshoe crabs move toward shallow water where they begin the spawning process. Males attach themselves to females and the couples (literally) come up into the surf zone where eggs are deposited in nests. Spawning sites have unique substrate characteristics that are not completely understood. In some coastal northern states, beaches become covered with spawning horseshoe crabs. The eggs hatch and the larvae eventually take up life on the bottom.

Food and products for many

Coastal Indians in South Carolina used the tail of the horseshoe crab as a spear point. More recently, horseshoe crabs are caught and used for bait, but this is not now allowed in South Carolina. The blood of horseshoe crabs has a unique chemical that indicates the presence of bacterial contamination. Biomedical companies purchase the crabs from fishermen, bleed them, and then return the animals to the wild. Finally, the eggs of horseshoe crabs make up an important and highly nutritious component of the diets of various shore birds. Unfortunately, as is the case with most harvested marine creatures, horseshoe crab populations are on the decline. Research is underway in South Carolina to identify and protect critical spawning sites.

Don't disturb the parents

If mating pairs of horseshoe crabs are discovered, keep your distance and don't disturb them. Such mating events are not common along the Grand Strand and any interruption could lead to reduced egg production. Report the event to the Department of Natural Resources at 1 800 861-8270.

See also: blue crab, ghost crab, gull, loggerhead sea turtle

Jellyfish

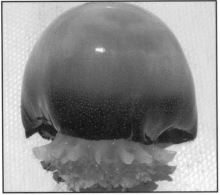

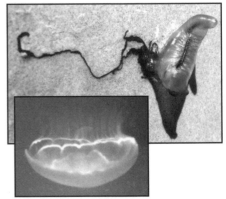

Cannonball jellyfish do not generally sting. (above)   The long stinging tentacles of the Portuguese man-o-war can stretch 10 to 15 feet from the colorful float. (top right)   Moon jellies occur off the beach, mostly in the winter. (lower right)

Zoology 102

Jellyfish belong to a group of marine invertebrate animals that are relatively simple in their body structures. All members of the group, including sea anemones and corals, at some point in their life cycles take on a body form that is round. This round stage of the life cycle is known as the medusa. In jellyfish, the medusa moves with the wind and the current as it swims. These creatures with no bones, brains, or well-developed internal organs, are found around the world. Some have tentacles with stinging cells and toxins while others are harmless. The tentacles gather food, which is then moved to a primitive, one-holed stomach. Jellyfish feed on plankton, small fish, and other jellyfish.

Beach jellies (no sting)

Beachcombers and boaters along the Grand Strand will most likely encounter the cannonball jelly. It is white or bluish with brown bands and is hemispherical. The tough ball is usually less than 8 inches in diameter. Cannonball jellyfish feed with a cluster of ragged, short arms. They have no tentacles and do not sting! At certain times of the year, cannonball jellyfish cover the beach where they are picked to pieces by gulls, ghost crabs, and curious children. Cannonball jellyfish are gathered and used as bait for catching Atlantic spadefish. The moon jellyfish is another common jellyfish that gets up to 16 inches in diameter. Despite its size it is not considered dangerous.

Beach jellies (stingers)

When stinging jellyfish are present, lifeguards will usually issue a warning. However, all beach visitors should recognize the species that do cause problems. Along the Grand Strand beware of the jellyfish with long or string-like tentacles. The lion's mane jellyfish, with eight clusters of tentacles, is present during cold months. The Portuguese man-of-war, with its purple float and tentacles extending to 50 feet, sometimes drifts into our area. The Portuguese man-of-war is not a true jellyfish but this point is not important to someone experiencing the intense pain and side effects of the stinging cells. Two other stinging jellyfish are the sea wasp (box-shaped with tentacles hanging from the corner) and the sea nettle (round with marginal tentacles).

Sting solutions

Depending on the species involved and the area of contact, human reactions to jellyfish stings can range from minor rash to death. The same can be said for bee stings. Follow these suggestions and jellyfish problems will be minimized. Don't touch beached jellyfish of the stinging varieties. As long as the tentacles are wet they can still sting. If you are in the water and see a floating jellyfish, remember that the tentacles can extend far from the medusa. If you get stung, leave the water quickly and find a lifeguard. So that venom injection in minimized, the lifeguard will carefully remove the tentacles, and will also likely apply vinegar, meat tenderizer, or baking soda. In the rare event of a severe allergic reaction, get to a hospital as soon as possible.

See also: ghost crab, gull, loggerhead sea turtle

Knobbed Whelk

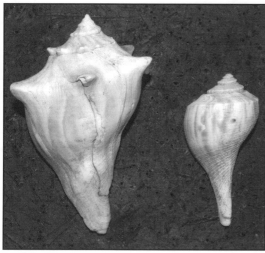

Knobbed Whelk shells are among the largest shells on Grand Strand beaches.

The Channelled whelk is similar to the knobbed whelk, but with a groove along the shell's spiral.

Whelk egg case.

A shell worth finding

Although Grand Strand beaches are not known for good shell collecting, occasionally the right combination of wind and tide will bring in large deposits of clams and snails. At these times, visitors actively collect the shells of the knobbed whelk. This snail is preferred because the shell is large (up to 10 inches) with a characteristic right-handed spiral that is reminiscent of conchs found in warmer climates. The bumps on the edge of the spiral provide the common name. The channeled whelk is similar to the knobbed whelk but lacks knobs and instead has a groove along the spiral. If you find a knobbed whelk on the beach, check to determine if the animal is live or dead. If a knobbed whelk is alive the tough operculum will be pulled up inside the shell but still visible. Live snails should be returned to the water.

Necklaces of eggs

Although live knobbed whelks are relatively rare on the beach, many beachcombers have encountered the string of egg capsules produced by female knobbed whelks. These strings are attached to the substrate and each string represents days of egg-laying efforts. Knobbed whelks are unique in that these eggs hatch directly into small, fully formed whelks.

A predator of the mud

Knobbed whelks move along the bottom in shallow waters where they feed primarily on clams and oysters. They pry open the shells and then insert a proboscis that sucks out the flesh. In some parts of the Atlantic coast knobbed whelks are the most important bottom predator.

Catching whelks

Although knobbed whelks are not a commercially important species in South Carolina, they are sometimes harvested during collection of oysters, clams and even crabs. In Georgia, shrimp fishermen in the off-season trawl for whelks using nets that scrape along the bottom. The snails are marketed primarily as conch although this is not quite truthful. A dish known as scungilli is made from the flesh of the knobbed whelk.

See also: hard clam, lettered olive, moon snail, oyster

Largemouth Bass

Bass fishing at the beach

Thousands of avid bass fishermen visit the Grand Strand each year. When these anglers see freshwater, they immediately begin thinking about bass potential. However, fishermen attuned to big, deep lakes will need to make some adjustments. Two types of bass habitat are available along the Grand Strand: small ponds and the Waccamaw River. The many golf course, subdivision, and storm water detention ponds occurring along the Grand Strand offer the best chance for consistently catching big bass. Fish in the 4-5 pound class are common in these small impoundments. The Waccamaw River and the sloughs leading into it are also bass habitat, but low oxygen and flow conditions tend to limit fish sizes and numbers. In the lower Waccamaw River veteran bass anglers target the cuts that allow water to move in and out of old rice fields. Bass congregate in the cuts and ambush bait fish as they are swept out of the rice fields.

Go shallow

Grand Strand bass fishing is a shallow water game. Few ponds exceed 6 feet in depth; Waccamaw bass are taken primarily from near bald cypress trees, from floating or emergent vegetation, or in shallow cuts along the bank. Buzz baits and surface poppers work well. Small spinnerbaits can be good. However, a live bluegill hooked under a slip bobber is the best. Contrary to big lakes where bass feed early and late, Grand Strand bass can be caught throughout the day. This is likely the result of the abundance of cover and the naturally dark color of the water. If possible, target subdivision ponds as these are more likely to be stocked by people living near the lakes. Bass in these ponds feed almost entirely on sunfish.

Big bass can be caught in most Grand Strand ponds.

On the beds

Largemouth bass along the Grand Strand begin showing spawning behavior in March. The onset of spawning is indicated by big fish moving into relatively shallow waters. At this time, groups of fish can be seen cruising along the edges of ponds. Smaller males eventually stop moving and sweep out beds in water that is usually about a foot deep. Bigger females deposit eggs and then the males guard the nests until the eggs hatch. In clear water, clouds of newly hatched bass can be observed near the beds. As in other parts of the country, bass on the beds are less likely to take lures. Indeed, to assure future bass populations, bedding bass should not be harassed.

Catch and release

Bass grow big along the Grand Strand, but they also pick up relatively high levels of mercury in the tissues due to natural abundance of this element. Do not eat the bass that you catch.

See also: bowfin, bream, storm water detention pond, Waccamaw National Wildlife Refuge

Lettered Olive

Lettered olives are most commonly found just below the tide's edge at night.

A favorite find

The lettered olive is a cylindrical snail that gets nearly 3 inches long. It has a highly polished surface with crisscrossed lines that resemble primitive letters and two broad bands of dark coloration. The conical part of the lettered olive ends in a point. Generally, gray or brown, the snail is a prize among those who comb the beaches looking for elegant shells.

Olive ecology

Not much is known about this bottom dweller. It apparently spends most of its time just under the surface of the sand. Here it extends its foot and covers the shell for protection. It is a predator that feeds on small invertebrates. Coquina are a favorite food item of the lettered olive. After it captures a coquina, it drags the victim under the sand and then surrounds it with the foot. Eventually the coquina opens and the meat is consumed.

The State Shell

The lettered olive is the State Shell of South Carolina. It was first described by Dr. Edmund Ravenel, a prolific scientist who lived in Charleston and devoted his life to the study and description of mollusks.

See also: coquina, knobbed whelk, moon snail, oyster drill

Loggerhead sea turtle 34

(left) Loggerhead sea turtles usually nest at night. This one however began too late and was caught after sunrise at Huntington Beach State Park

(top) Baby loggerheads face many dangers before they grow large enough to be safe from marine predators.

The state reptile

Visitors to the Grand Strand can consider themselves lucky nature watchers if they see a loggerhead sea turtle or even if they see evidence of one. Although this is the state reptile, population sizes in South Carolina are on the decline and the Grand Strand does not experience a lot of nesting activity. The loggerhead is so named because of the rough plates that cover its thick head. It has a stout beak used for crushing crabs, clams, horseshoe crabs, and mussels. Full-grown adults have shells about 3 feet long and may weigh 300 pounds.

Turtles on the beach

During most of their adult lives, loggerhead sea turtles roam the open oceans. However, during summer, females crawl up on the beaches and deposit eggs in nests. It takes 12 or more years before a female reaches a stage where egg production is possible. Nests are usually excavated at the base of dunes where the sand is relatively loose and well drained. Each nest contains about 100 eggs. In 60 days the eggs hatch and the hatchlings scurry toward the water. A female may lay two to four clutches of eggs in a season. Nesting occurs only at night. Artificial lighting, like that associated with resorts, will cause females to go elsewhere. This is why visitors to the Grand Strand see those bumper stickers encouraging "lights out" along the beach.

Turtle troubles

Several factors likely contribute to listing of the loggerhead sea turtle as a threatened species. For many years, thousands of turtles were caught in shrimp trawl nets and subsequently drowned. However, this mortality is now reduced as a result of special devices that exclude the turtles. Beach nourishment (sand dumping), human trampling, and off-road vehicle traffic may destroy nests or negatively change the substrate composition. Any structure that protects a beach from wave erosion will likely stop turtle nesting. During summer 2002, extremely high tides and strong winds caused erosion of a large dune area at Huntington Beach State Park. Two loggerhead turtle nests were lost during that time.

Helping the turtles

Volunteers throughout South Carolina are involved in activities that improve loggerhead sea turtle nesting success. They watch for turtle tracks and then mark the nests so the eggs will not be disturbed. If a nest is threatened the eggs are carefully moved to a new site. When the hatchlings emerge, volunteers facilitate the march to the sea by warding off predators such as raccoons and ghost crabs.

See also: blue crab, hard clam, horseshoe crab, Huntington Beach State Park

Moon snail

Neat round holes suggest the work of a predatory snail.

The body of the live moon snail extends out and around the shell opening.

Moon snails lay their eggs in a collar shaped egg mass.

What is it?

The moon snail is a relatively large (about 3 inches high) snail that lives from the intertidal zone to deeper waters. The smooth, round shells of moon snails are commonly found on Grand Strand beaches. In life, the muscular foot is several times larger than the shell. This is a predatory species feeding primarily on clams and other snails. It finds its prey by sliding through the sand and mud.

Making a clam milkshake

Moon snails feed by drilling neat round holes in the shells of clams. Indeed, moon snails are sometimes referred to as clam drills. If you find a clam shell with a hole, chances are high that a moon snail was involved. The hole is drilled with a toothed rasp-like structure that also secretes acid. Once the hole is made the moon snail injects digestive juices into the clams and then sucks out the thick liquid. Moon snails are active predators and can have strong effects on the numbers of clams living in shallow waters.

What about those round things on the beach?

During spring, beach combers may occasionally find a strange object on the beach that looks something like the inner tube of a small wheel. This is a sand collar. It is produced by the moon snail as a case for the eggs. The sand collar is secreted continuously, but it eventually assumes the rounded shape of the muscular foot. The eggs hatch and the larvae emerge as microscopic plankton.

Can I eat them?

Moon snails in some parts of the world are eaten and the flesh is considered quite good. However, beach combers will not often be presented with live moon snails except when high winds and tides deposit them on the beach.

See also: hard clam, knobbed whelk, oyster, oyster drill

Mosquito

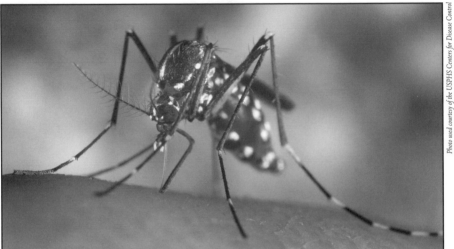

Several varieties of mosquitoes inhabit the Grand Strand. All are regarded as pests and some can potentially carry diseases.

Mosquito matters

Although Grand Strand mosquitoes are not nearly as numerous as in northern states, they can be a problem particularly at dusk. Indeed, considering the large areas of standing water, it is surprising that mosquitoes are not more of a problem. However, there may be natural factors in our area that keep them under control. Many of our small ponds are populated by mosquito fish that consume the larvae. Sandy soils may also contribute to quick drainage of water from all but low-lying areas. Mosquitoes lay their eggs in stagnant water, and the wiggling larvae are aquatic. When adults emerge, the females must take a blood meal every several days. It is the females that bite and they live for about 2 weeks. Mosquitoes reproduce repeatedly during the warm months.

Mosquitoes and South Carolina history

Mosquitoes, and the diseases they carry, have shaped several aspects of South Carolina history. Rice planta-tions that emerged along the coastal rivers in the 1700's were prime breeding grounds for mosquitoes and the associated malaria and yellow fever transmitted by them. Slaves that worked the rice fields were less susceptible to these diseases, although slaves suffered from other hardships. Plantation owners and their families, however, were very susceptible and mortality was high. In response, most plantation owners left the plantations during the "fever" months and took up residence elsewhere. These absentee landlords could not live year round in the region that produced for them great wealth.

Mosquitoes and West Nile Virus

Beginning in 1999 a new mosquito-transmitted disease called West Nile virus (WNV) was reported in New York. Since that time the disease has spread to most states and in 2002 WNV was reported in South Carolina. The virus infects and kills birds. Other animals may also be infected. When mosquitoes feed on infected birds the virus can be transmitted to humans. West Nile virus produces no symptoms, mild flu-like symptoms, or seri-ous flu-like symptoms and rarely can lead to death. However, risks as of 2002 in the Grand Strand area were low due to the extremely low number of infected birds and the low number of infected mosquitoes. This situation could change in the future. Still, it is best to avoid mosquito bites by staying indoors at dusk, by wearing long-sleeved shirts and long pants, and by applying mosquito repellent. Mosquito reproduction sites such as old tires, bird baths, and clogged gutters should be eliminated. In summer 2001 Horry County began both on-ground and aerial spraying for mosquitoes.

See also: flies, freshwater wetland, mosquito fish, rice field, tick

Mosquito Fish

Female mosquito fish (above) is larger than the tiny males (below).

Pond guppies

Mosquito fish, ubiquitous in ponds and streams of the Grand Strand, are the first fish to appear in new bodies of water. These are the small fish that hover at the water surface in shaded vegetation near the shore. When frightened they scatter and make small ripples at the surface. Mosquito fish can be easily captured with a dip net. They look like guppies but have no bright coloration. Females, larger than males, are olive-colored, and when pregnant, have a distinct dark spot at the rear of the belly. Males are yellowish, and the rear fin carries a small reproductive organ. Both males and females have a dark stripe through the eye and the lower jaw slants upward.

Getting more mosquito fish

Mosquito fish, like guppies, give birth to live young. These baby fish develop in the mother for 5-8 weeks. Each female may produce 10-80 offspring. When born, they swim to the surface and fill their swim bladders with air. Young mosquito fish must move quickly to safe areas as the adults will eat the offspring.

A controversial mosquito control

Many books and papers describe the usefulness of the mosquito fish as a mosquito control agent. Mosquito fish live in the areas where mosquito larvae thrive and, because mosquito fish are active predators, they likely consume many mosquito larvae. Government agencies have introduced mosquito fish around the world in efforts to control mosquitoes and the diseases associated with mosquitoes. However, recent evidence suggests that introduced mosquito fish have strong impacts on native fish species. Furthermore, introduced mosquito fish may be no better than native fish in cropping down the mosquito populations.

Mosquito fish in the aquarium

Mosquito fish make good aquarium specimens. They are hardy and can tolerate a wide range of water conditions. They will reproduce in captivity. However, they are aggressive and will do battle with each other and with other species in the same tank.

See also: bowfin, bream, flathead catfish, largemouth bass, mosquito

Mud minnow

The Mummichug is commonly sold for bait as the mud minnow.

Striped killifish are a different species, but are often mixed in with mud minnows.

Up north it's mummichog

The mud minnow is the dominant small fish of salt marshes. It is recognized by white patches on the fins and vertical, zigzag gold lines along the body. These fish get up to 5 inches, but 2 to 3 inches is typical along the Grand Strand. Here in the south the species is called the mud minnow, but as you go north the common name shifts to mummichog. The mud minnow belongs to a large group of fish known as killifish and indeed, another species, the striped killifish may be found along with mud minnows.

A day in the life

Mud minnows move in the marsh with the tides. As the tide comes in, schools of mud minnows follow small creeks and eventually make their way into the stands of smooth cordgrass. Here they feed on invertebrates and dead bits of plants, and also lay their eggs. Mud minnows may affect many marsh processes due to their appetites and high population numbers. As the tide goes out, one will often see mud minnows moving in very shallow waters as they make their way back to the creeks. Sometimes they get stranded in isolated pools, but these are tough fish and unless they are eaten by birds, they will likely survive until the next high tide.

Lab fish

Mud minnows tolerate waters ranging from fresh to highly saline. Their unique physiology is widely studied in efforts to understand how they deal with the different environments. Because they are constant components of salt marshes, they are also used in efforts to monitor the impacts of various types of pollutants.

Good bait

Mud minnows are the bait of choice for flounder and red drum. Flounder fishermen use rigs that allow mud minnows to be slowly trolled just off the bottom. Red drum fishermen use large slip bobbers and float mud minnows across oyster beds and near jetties. Mud minnows can be caught by placing minnow traps in small marsh creeks. Most people, however, make a trip to the bait store.

See also: flounder, mullet, pinfish, red drum, salt marsh

Mullet

Large schools of striped mullet are found in the Atlantic.

Those jumping fish

Mullet are torpedo-shaped fish that occur in large schools. Individual fish frequently jump from the water. Although several species of mullet occur in coastal waters of the Grand Strand, the most common one is the striped mullet. It has a cylindrical body, blunt nose, upturned mouth, and 6-7 parallel stripes along the sides. Many other common names are applied to this fish because it has a world-wide distribution: black, sea, gray. However, in our area, fishermen use two names: finger mullet refers to striped mullets less than 6 inches long; horse mullet refers to striped mullets longer than 6 inches. Indeed, striped mullets can get up to 18 inches long. Striped mullet swim along the beach, offshore, in estuaries, and can even move up into freshwater rivers

Mullet maneuvers

Striped mullets move offshore during fall to spawn in large schools. It may take 3 years of growth in coastal waters before females are large enough to make this spawning run. Larvae are transported to coastal waters. After the first year of life, the juveniles are able to move into many different habitats. As mullet increase in size, their diet shifts from small crustaceans to small plants. They get these plants at the surface of the water, at the surface of other large plants, or by sifting through the sediments.

Baiting up

The striped mullet is pursued by a wide variety of birds and fish. Not surprisingly, it is the preferred bait of offshore and inshore fishermen. Lures and flies have been produced to simulate this species. Live mullet can be caught with cast nets and this casting is best done when the schools of fish are tightly packed. Finger mullet caught in the tidal creeks can be used live for flounder and sea trout. Dead mullet, presented whole or cut in chunks, is prime bait for big bluefish. Mullet are bait but they also make tasty table fare either eaten smoked or fried. Striped mullet are netted commercially during fall, and the eggs are sold in European and Asian markets.

Cast netting for mullet.

What about that jumping?

Visitors to the Grand Strand are frequently treated to the spectacle of individual jumping mullets. It occurs just off the beach and in tidal creeks; jumping striped mullet often surprise bass fishermen working the shallow sloughs of local rivers. Each fish makes a series of jumps and then disappears. Scientists think that this may be a way of getting oxygen after the fish have spent some time feeding near the bottom. Of course, when whole schools of mullet jump from the water this means that predatory fish are in pursuit. At these times it is best to get out the fishing pole and cast lures that imitate the mullet.

See also: bluefish, flounder, Atlantic menhaden, mud minnow, sea trout

Osprey

Osprey on its nest along the Intracoastal Waterway. (above)   An abandoned osprey nest. (inset)

Fish hawk of the Grand Strand

One of the most common predatory birds of the Grand Strand is the osprey. In all but the coldest months of the year, this bird is readily observed along rivers and in marshes. Ospreys are dark brown above and white below. They have a characteristic dark mask across the eyes. Any medium size hawk-like bird in the process of fishing will likely be an osprey.

Fishing gear

Fish make up nearly the entire diet of the osprey. The birds build their nests near shallow waters where fishing by sight is most successful. They soar and hover in search of prey. When a fish is spotted they plunge feet first into the water and then carry the catch to a place where it can be consumed. The talons on the feet are spiny to ensure a good grip on slippery fish. Oily feathers shed water. Osprey can grab and transport fish that far exceed the lengths of the feet.

Osprey of the Waccamaw

Numerous nesting pairs of osprey can be seen up close during a boating trip on the Waccamaw River. The birds prefer to build their nests in the veteran bald cypress trees that occur regularly at the edge of the bottomland forest. Because nests are used repeatedly they are large and can often occupy the entire upper areas of the trees. When parked in the vicinity of an osprey nest one can watch birds actively fishing and fighting. You can really hear them calling. The sounds can be quite loud especially when males are bringing fish to the young.

Snow birds

Osprey populations in South Carolina are migratory. During the cold months of the year they move to warmer climates and may wander as far as South America. However, they return to the Grand Strand in late winter and immediately begin the process of nest repair.

See also: freshwater wetland, double-crested cormorant, Sandy Island, Waccamaw National Wildlife Refuge

Oyster

Oyster bed. (above)   Bags of empty shells provide new oyster habitat. (top right)
Oyster clump. (bottom right)

A key animal of tidal creeks

Oysters are filter feeders related to clams and mussels. In South Carolina most oysters are found in areas influenced by tidal fluctuations. They thrive in both brackish and saltwater. A single oyster may pump and process as much as 100 gallons of water each day. Small particles of food are trapped by the gills and are then funneled to the stomach. This mode of feeding can influence water quality and the types of microscopic organisms in the water. Indeed, the extremely clear waters that once existed in major estuaries of the east coast were likely the result of extensive oyster beds and their concerted filtering of the water.

Settling down

Larval oysters known as "spat" will settle and attach to hard substrates. A preferred substrate is oyster shell. Thus, colonies of oysters grow through time with young oysters settling on top of old oysters. Oysters on the bottom of the stack will suffocate, but the remaining shells serve an important function. Oyster beds are used by many different species. Other invertebrates use the beds for spawning and for hiding. The beds also stabilize sediments and protect the salt marsh from erosion. Sport fish frequent oyster beds as these hold small bait fish.

Making more beds

As in many parts of the east coast, oyster populations in South Carolina have declined through time. These declines are related to pollution and over harvest. Availability of substrate for the larvae was identified as a limiting factor and thus a program was started to fix this problem. The South Carolina Oyster Restoration and Enhancement program gathers oyster shells from restaurants and then recycles the shells into substrate. Citizen volunteers place shells in mesh bags and then deposit the bags in tidal creeks. These artificial beds will hopefully serve as future settling sites for oyster larvae. As a matter of good ecological practice, oyster shells should be returned to the tidal creeks. Many oystering areas near the Grand Strand have been closed due to pollution. Check the state regulations before gathering oysters in the wild.

Early oyster roasting

Indians living on the coast of South Carolina were very much dependent on oysters as food. They consumed so many oysters that large piles of discarded shells are still visible today. These piles called "middens" include very large oyster shells as well as mussels and fish bones. Mysterious features known as shell rings occur along the southern coast of South Carolina. These circles of shells were constructed by Indians, but the function of the shell rings is not known. Construction of new shell rings ceased about 2000 years ago, and the structures were left to nature.

See also: blue crab, Huntington Beach State Park, mud minnow, oyster drill, red drum

Oyster Drill

A snail with a tool

The Atlantic oyster drill is a predatory snail occurring in estuaries and in shallow shore waters. It is an oval-shaped, gray snail that can grow to about 2 inches in length. An oyster drill is recognized by its bumpy, ribbed shell. There are usually five whorls and the lip or outer edge of the shell is thin and sharp. The tool of the oyster drill is a toothed structure called a radula. The oyster drill uses this like a file to bore neat, round holes in the shells of oysters, clams, and barnacles. Once a hole is complete, a feeding structure is inserted through the hole and the meat of the prey item is sucked out. This method of predation is similar to that used by the moon snail. Examine the clam shells you find on the beach. Most of them have holes representing the craftsmanship of predatory snails.

Oysters and oyster drills

In oyster beds, the oyster drill is an active predator. It feeds preferably on young oysters and may cause high rates of mortality. Where oysters are cultivated, oyster growers attempt to eradicate oysters drills by removing them from the growing area. Growers also enclose oysters in cages as a way of excluding oyster drills.

Oyster drills on the move

The oyster drill is not a very mobile animal. It lays its eggs in small cases that are attached to the substrate and the larvae emerge as crawlers rather than as floaters. However, the range of the oyster drill is constantly increasing. The species was originally limited to New England waters but it is now found down the east coast and on the west coast and has also invaded waters around Great Britain. Apparently, as eastern oysters were transported to various parts of the world to supply oyster growers, the oyster drill hitched a ride. This is just one more example of how people can inadvertently introduce new species into new environments.

See also: oyster, knobbed whelk, moon snail, ribbed mussel

Pen Shell

Rigid pen shell. (top)   Sawtooth pen shell. (bottom)

Beach fan

The pen shell is a fan- or wedge-shaped clam. The shell is thin and fragile and partial pieces are often found on Grand Strand beaches. The outer surface of the shell is dark green or black, but the inside surface is glossy pink or purple. Pen shells thrive in shallow near-shore waters. They partially bury themselves in the sand and then attach to the substrate with a tangle of thread-like strands. As is the case with many attached mollusks, pen shells are filter feeders. Two species of pen shell are found on Grand Strand beaches. The saw-toothed pen shell is covered with scales and has about 30 ridges. The rigid pen shell is covered with short spines.

The pen shell as habitat

Pen shells are relatively large and flat. This shell structure is used by several other organisms. Living pen shells often harbor small crabs inside. It is assumed that these crabs feed on the particles of food taken into the pen shell. When pen shells die, the shells provide hard substrate that is quickly colonized by other invertebrates. Larval fish seek shelter under and inside the shells.

Golden fleece from pen shells

A large species of pen shell occurring off the coast of Italy was historically harvested for its long attachment threads. These threads known as "sea silk" were sown into cloth. The mythical golden fleece sought by Jason and the Argonauts is rumored to be made from sea silk.

See also: coquina, hard clam, oyster, ribbed mussel

Pinfish

Sunfish of the sea

Pinfish are perhaps the most numerous and the most easily caught saltwater fish in the Grand Strand area. Although they occur in greatest numbers in shallow waters near vegetation, pinfish are commonly caught from piers, in the surf, and even while fishing deep holes offshore. They are recognized by the alternating blue and yellow stripes and by the dark spot just behind the gill plate. Most pinfish caught in shallow waters are less then 9 inches long, although they can get up to 15 inches.

Attack of the bait stealers

Fishermen often curse pinfish because they attack baits intended for other species. Indeed, if you toss a shrimp in the water and numerous bites produce nothing but an empty hook, the culprit is likely a school of pinfish. If nothing else is biting, switch to a very small hook and enjoy the pinfish bite. Although they are not regularly eaten by the locals, they do put up a good fight. Do not confuse pinfish with spots. Spots have mouths more suited to bottom feeding and they are avidly pursued by fishermen because of their good taste.

Pinfish importance

Although pinfish are not respected by fishermen, they do deserve respect for their ecological roles. Specifically, pinfish are a major component of flounder and red drum diets. Pinfish themselves consume many different food items, including vegetation. Thus they serve as a important link in transferring plant energy to larger fish. This role is significant due to high pinfish populations. Pinfish are unique in that they shift to plant-based diets as they get larger.

A bait fish

Fisherman searching for bluefish, flounder, red drum, and sea trout, must often rely on pinfish as bait. They are used live or cut into long strips. Many a fishing trip in the Grand Strand area has been salvaged when the last remaining bait shrimp were put on small hooks and then used to catch pinfish.

See also: bluefish, flounder, red drum, Winyah Bay Fishing and Observation Pier.

Polychaete worm

Clam worm, one of many polychaetes.

Zoology 101

The mud of estuaries and the intertidal zone along the Grand Strand is home to a large variety of invertebrates. One type of invertebrate in this habitat, known as the polychaete worm, is characterized by the presence of numerous paired bristles called parapodia. The parapodia are used for digging in the mud and for moving across the bottom. Polychaete worms represent a diverse group of bottom-dwelling marine worms that feed by different methods. Visitors to the Grand Strand will likely encounter blood worms, clam worms and lugworms.

Great bait

The blood worm is a predator of soft bottoms. It remains buried except for the head. As prey items pass by, the blood worm shoots out a clawed proboscis that grabs and also injects a mild toxin. Prey are then pulled back down into the mud and eaten. Blood worms live in mud flats along the Grand Strand. However, visitors will most likely encounter them for sale in bait stores. Specifically, blood worms are the preferred bait for catching spots in the fall. The pricey blood worms sold in bait stores likely come from Maine where mud flats are extensive and where harvest occurs on a large scale. When handling them, beware of the proboscis. It will shoot out and cause a painful bite. Clam worms live in sturdy tubes but emerge from the tubes at night to search for prey.

Eating mud

The lugworm lives in a tube-shaped burrow where it feeds on sediment. It is an indiscriminate feeder and thus must process large quantities of sediments in order to gain some useful food items. In one day, lugworms may consume up to ten times their own weight in sediment. After chowing down on the mud, the lugworm discards the unused material at the opening of its burrow. These piles of worm poop are common along the beach.

Moving mud

Scientists who study bottom-dwelling critters stress the importance of lugworms and other deposit feeders in a process called bioturbation. Here animals are implicated in moving sediments from one place (deep in the mud) to another place (the surface). Such moving and sorting brings nutrients back to the water where they can be used by plants and microbes.

See also: fiddler crab, hard clam, sea star

Red Drum

Red drum or spottail bass are highly regarded as a food and sports fish. (top) Jetties provide good fishing for red drum. (bottom)

With a spot on the tail

Red drum are members of the drum family and thus share with spot and Atlantic croaker the characteristic over-hanging upper jaw. They have bronze backs and a distinctive dark spot at the base of the tail. In some individuals, there may be several tail spots. Red drum are also known as channel bass or spottail bass. They have special status among sport fishermen because they get big, they hit a variety of artificial baits including flies, and they put up a re-spectable fight when hooked. Unfortunately, red drum over harvest in the past likely contributed to declining stocks. The species is now under special slot limits, and restocking is done in an effort to rebuild the populations.

Drum ecology

Red drum are ready to reproduce when they are 3-4 years old. At this age, they are about 2 feet long. Rebuilding red drum populations requires conservation of the big fish. Spawning of these big fish occurs offshore in fall. The larvae, as with many coastal fish, ride the tidal currents into the estuaries. Juveniles live in the tidal creeks and estuaries where they move with the tides. High tide finds them foraging for crabs in the smooth cordgrass. Low tide finds them foraging for shrimp and mud minnows in the creeks and near oyster beds. As the juveniles increase in size, they progressively move toward deeper inlets and near-shore areas.

Drum in winter

One of the major predators of juvenile red drum is the bottlenose dolphin. In winter, red drum seek protection from these large fish-eaters by moving into very shallow creeks. Unfortunately, these same shallow waters also experience low temperatures during extended cold spells. When water temperatures drop below the mid 40's for several days, the fish get very lethargic and may even die due to stress. Winter mortality is an important factor in the size of red drum populations.

Catching drum

Red drum are caught with a variety of approaches. The big fish (20 – 30 pounds) are pursued in deep water near the inlets with heavy rods and cut bait. Near the jetties, mud minnows under float rigs work well. In the tidal creeks, shrimp are used as bait and are tossed to the edge of the cordgrass or near oyster beds. Here also, float rigs serve to keep the bait from snagging. During winter when the water is clear, fly fishermen and jig fishermen sight cast to red drum as they forage through the shallows. Although current regulations allow the harvest of two fish within the slot limit (15 – 24 inches) fishermen should strive for safe catch and total release.

See also: Atlantic croaker, bottlenose dolphin, mud minnow, shrimp, smooth cordgrass, spot

Ribbed Mussel

Ribbed muscles live among oyster reefs and in salt marshes.

Mussel matters

Mussels are mollusks typically found attached to various substrates in salt marshes and on mud flats. The ribbed mussel is identified by the parallel raised lines extending from the hinge to the outer edges of the shell. Generally, the gray shell is fan-shaped. There is a hinge on the front, top side of the mussel; on the front, bottom side there are thread-like structures that attach to the substrate. In some salt marshes, the mass of mussels may equal or exceed that of oysters.

Mussel feeding

Like many of the mollusks, mussels are filter feeders. They process large volumes of water; particles of food riding the mussel-generated current are trapped by the gills. This filtering function can be substantial when mussel beds extend across entire salt marshes.

Mussel benefits

Mussels, like oysters, are important engineers in the salt marsh. Their attachment threads known as byssal threads help to bind and stabilize sediments. Ribbed mussels may even reposition their byssal threads as a mechanism for pulling themselves deeper in the mud. Ribbed mussels excrete waste products that in turn stimulate the growth of adjacent smooth cordgrass. The mussel shells also provide habitat for small crabs and juvenile fish.

Dental benefits from mussels

Mussels produce a powerful adhesive that binds byssal threads to various substrates. This adhesive continues to function under harsh environmental conditions. Researchers are at work characterizing this adhesive because it may have some applications in dentistry.

See also: barnacle, hard clam, moon snail, oyster, oyster drill

Salt Marsh Periwinkle 48

Salt marsh periwinkles often climb cordgrass stalks.

What are they?

Put on your mud shoes and take a hike into the salt marsh. If it is high tide and the cordgrass is abundant, you will see thousands of snails clinging to the cordgrass stems. These are salt marsh periwinkles, the most numerous and conspicuous animal of the marsh. They occur from the mid-Atlantic states to the Gulf of Mexico. As many as 70 periwinkles have been counted in a single square foot of land, although about 10 per square foot of marsh is more likely.

What do they do?

Periwinkles feed by scraping. They do this with a file-like structure in the mouth called a radula. For many years scientists thought that the scraping was confined to dead plant tissues. However, recent research suggests that periwinkles also eat live plants. They wound the plant and then return to feed on the microbes (fungi, algae) infecting the wound. When populations of periwinkles get very high, they may even start to thin out the cordgrass as the plants succumb to repeated scraping and wounding.

What eats periwinkles?

When the tide comes in, salt marsh periwinkles climb up the stems of cordgrass. They do this to feed, but they also do this to escape their most common predator, the blue crab. The crabs are fast and agile while the periwinkles are painfully slow. Blue crabs can easily extract the soft tissue of the periwinkle, leaving behind hundreds of empty shells on the mud. These shells are buried in the sediments and eventually contribute to the substrate of salt marshes.

Where can I see them?

Huntington Beach State Park is the best place to observe salt marsh periwinkles. Take the marsh boardwalk all the way to the end. Here is where the cordgrass grows tall and periwinkles can be seen by the thousands.

See also: blue crab, smooth cordgrass, Huntington Beach State Park, salt marsh

Sanderling

Photo courtesy of Dr. Reginald Daves

Sanderlings are the common small sandpiper found along the water's edge.

A Bird of the beach

The sanderling is a small sandpiper that feeds on the beach. It has a black bill and black legs. The underside of the bird is white, but the top side is gray. Sanderlings are most commonly observed running back and forth in the surf zone. They chase the waves in efforts to capture small clams, worms, and crustaceans.

Probing and prying

The bill of the sanderling is pointed at the tip. It is well suited for probing in the sand and prying open small clams. Sanderlings constantly search for vulnerable coquina clams. When a coquina clam presents a slightly open shell, the sanderling can quickly wedge open the shell and then feed on the soft body.

Long-distance traveler

The sanderling has a world-wide distribution. It can be found on most beaches of the world. It also migrates long distances. Nesting areas are located in the Canadian arctic. These same birds may migrate in winter as far south as the southern tip of South America. Grand Strand sanderlings are most common during fall and winter.

A worrisome trend

Sanderling populations are regularly monitored at various points along the east coast. Some of these studies suggest that sanderling numbers are on the decline. Although the reasons for this trend are not clear, it may be that sanderlings are not able to feed as efficiently on beaches that support human activities. While it may be fun to herd the sanderlings along the beach, this disturbance may have subtle effects on their abilities to capture energy. It is best to not disturb them.

Other wading sand birds

In addition to the sanderling, a large variety of relatively small wading birds can be seen on or near the beach. The piping plover, willet, and various other sandpiper species are available for the hardcore birder, but correct identification requires binoculars, patience, and a good bird book.

See also: brown pelican, coquina, gull, willet.

Sea star

Sea star.

Sand dollar.

Sea urchin.

Zoology 101

Sea stars belong to a group of invertebrates known as echinoderms. The group also includes sea urchins and sand dollars. Sea stars are round with body parts in multiples of five. The Forbes' common sea star, with five arms, is the species most likely encountered by beachcombers along the Grand Strand. This animal will be found stranded in shallow tide pools at low tide. It is usually light tan, although it can be brown and in some cases even orange. On the upper side of the sea star is a prominent round spot called the madreporite. This serves as an entry point for water circulating through the sea star body. On the lower side are grooves lined with special structures called tube feet. These are used for movement and for applying suction to various prey items. The tips of the arms have small light-sensing spots. Sand dollars are flat and the five arms are fused to form a disc. Sea urchins are round and are typically covered with spines.

A slow but persistent predator

The Forbes' common sea star preys on barnacles and mollusks (i.e., clams, mussels, oysters). In some parts of the country where mollusks are cultured and harvested, the sea star is a nuisance and is subject to eradication efforts. Sea stars wrap their arms around prey and apply a strong, consistent pull. Research shows that the force applied by seas stars exceeds the opposite force exerted by most mollusks. When prey items open only slightly, sea stars insert their stomachs between the shells and secrete digestive enzymes. The thick molluskan soup is then conveyed to the mouth of the sea star.

A key species

In some areas of North America where the subtidal zone is rocky rather than sandy, sea stars play an important role by preying on mollusks. They are the top predator and can actually limit mollusk distribution and abundance. When sea stars are removed from the system or when sea star populations plummet, mollusk populations expand.

Tossed on the beach

Many sea stars, sand dollars, and sea urchins are found on the beach after a storm or when storms coincide with high tides. Storm tossing may be one of the greatest sources of early mortality in these animals since few animals eat them when they are in the water. However, stranded sea stars make easy meals for gulls and ghost crabs.

See also: barnacle, hard clam, moon snail, oyster, oyster drill, ribbed mussel

Seatrout

The weakfish or summer trout. (bottom) The spotted seatrout or winter trout. (top)

Spots or not

Two species of seatrout are commonly caught along the Grand Strand: the spotted seatrout and the weakfish. Both are elongate, silver fish with relatively large delicate mouths and long teeth. The spotted seatrout has small distinct spots on the side; the weakfish is more uniformly silver on the sides with poorly defined speckles. Both are popular game fish that frequent the surf zone, inlets, and estuaries.

Seatrout ecology

Seatrout are highly dependent on estuaries for feeding, growing, and spawning. Spawning occurs in estuaries during the warm months. Females congregate in areas with current and with some type of bottom structure. They are attracted to spawning areas by the drumming sounds of males. Larvae ride the tidal currents into the marshes where they feed on small invertebrates. Juvenile fish remain in shallow areas and tidal creeks where they feed on shrimp and fish. As they increase in size, juveniles move to deeper creeks and the diet shifts more toward fish. Adult seatrout can remain in estuaries where they alternate between feeding on shallow flats and feeding at the edges of marshes. In summer, big seatrout may move to the beach where they feed on schools of migrating baitfish. Females can reproduce when they reach 10 inches in length. The current minimum size limit for keeping spotted seatrout is 13 inches. The size limit is set so that fish can complete at least one spawning cycle before they are harvested.

Catching trout

Summer and winter are the best times to fish for seatrout. During summer, big fish up to 5 pounds can be caught from piers and from the beach. Bottom rigs baited with shrimp or mud minnows are best. During winter, seatrout congregate in deep holes of the tidal creeks. At these times, when the water is clear, they can be caught with bait or small jigs. Fly fishermen pursue seatrout primarily when the fish move onto shallow flats. In Murrells Inlet the locals prefer slow trolling small green jigs near drop-offs and along creek channels.

Catch or keep?

Seatrout populations are on the decline throughout much of South Carolina. This trend is in place even though bag limits are generous (10 fish can be kept). It makes good sense to keep only one fish for the frying pan and then release the rest so spawning populations can increase. Such voluntary bag limits will go a long way toward improved fishing for all.

See also: Atlantic croaker, Atlantic menhaden, red drum, shrimp, spot

Shark

52

The small Atlantic sharpnose is the most common shark on the S.C. coast.

Bonnethead shark.

Blacktip shark

Sandbar shark.

The world's record tiger shark was caught off the Cherry Grove pier.

Sharks among us

Forty-one shark species are recognized and managed by the South Carolina Department of Natural Resources. Some of these sharks are open water animals that will not be encountered unless they are caught during deep-sea fishing trips. Others, however, are common in both shallow offshore and inshore areas along the Grand Strand. These can be experienced up close by hanging out at the jetties and fishing piers along the Grand Strand. Of the many wild things found in marine environments, sharks are perhaps the most misunderstood. They serve an important function as top predators in the marine ecosystem and should be protected. Catch and release should be practiced particularly because little is known about shark growth patterns and reproductive performance. However, in some parts of the country, sharks are captured solely to remove the dorsal fin that is sold in specialty markets. This type of harvest is likely to send some shark populations into steep declines.

The common ones

Sandbar, Atlantic sharpnose, and blacktip sharks are the common ones along the Grand Strand. On the beach and the piers, fishing for sharks is illegal. This Grand Strand law is in place to discourage attracting sharks to populated beach areas. However, it is difficult to demonstrate if and when someone fishing from a pier has intentionally or accidentally snagged a shark. The law is controversial and many arguments have erupted among anglers over the issue of catching sharks. Regardless of how a shark is caught, it should be unhooked and released. South of Georgetown, the bonnethead shark is actively pursued by recreational fishermen, but the pursuit of bonnetheads occurs in deep holes of the tidal creeks.

Shark teeth

Beachcombers spend much time searching the sand for fossilized shark teeth. The teeth are shiny black and can in some places be found in great numbers. Often, the best time to search is after high winds and tides have churned and sorted the beach sediments.

Shark bite

When people are bitten by sharks, this is big news. However, the risk of a shark bite is much lower than for other less newsworthy beach hazards such as drowning or jellyfish stings. Nearly all shark attacks in South Carolina are categorized as hit and run bites; sharks in murky waters mistake human limbs for natural prey. George Burgess of the Florida Museum of Natural History suggests the following in order to avoid shark bites: stay in a group, stay close to shore, avoid the water during darkness or twilight hours, do not swim if you are bleeding, don't swim in murky waters, don't swim when baitfish are visible, and avoid sandbars near deep drop-offs.

See also: blue crab, bluefish, dolphin, pinfish

Shrimp

Shrimp boats in Georgetown harbor.

Shrimp matters

For most visitors to the Grand Strand, shrimp come in three varieties: boiled, deep fried, or grilled. Biologists, however, identify three types of shrimp that may end up on the table: white shrimp, brown shrimp, and pink shrimp. Along the Grand Strand the majority of the commercial shrimp harvest is made up of white shrimp. These are light colored shrimp with black-edged tails. The tails of brown shrimp are edged in red or green. Pink shrimp are relatively rare. They have a red spot on the side of the body and the tails are bluish. Some veteran shrimp eaters claim they can distinguish by taste the three commercially important shrimp species. Other types of shrimp such as grass shrimp (found in tidal creeks) and rock shrimp (found offshore) are common but these are not often consumed by people.

Riding the tides

Because of the commercial importance of shrimp populations in South Carolina, much effort has been devoted to understanding the limits to the populations. Spawning of white shrimp occurs during spring in the open ocean. This is also when shrimp trawlers can be seen within a few miles of the beach. The eggs sink to bottom and eventually hatch into microscopic larvae. The larvae go through a series of developmental stages, eventually reaching a stage where they migrate into the estuaries. Migration is accomplished by rising to the surface when tidal currents move toward the estuaries and sinking to the bottom when tidal currents move away from the estuaries. Once settled in the mud of the tidal creeks, shrimp feed on anything that can be handled by their simple mouth parts. As the shrimp reach critical size in fall, they once again ride the tidal currents back out into the ocean. This timing of fall migration depends on rainfall and temperature. Fall also coincides with an increase in offshore trawler activity.

Baiting your own

During the fall, hundreds of Grand Strand residents participate in a unique sport called shrimp baiting. This method of catching shrimp involves setting a series of long poles in the tidal creeks. Shrimp bait such as fishmeal is mixed with clay, packed into balls, and then tossed near the poles. As the balls gradually decay, the bait is released and shrimp are attracted to the areas. The purpose of the poles is to mark the specific spots where bait is placed. A cast net is then used to catch the shrimp that swarm to the bait. Baiting greatly improves the efficiency of catching shrimp with a cast net. Shrimp baiting is also tightly regulated in terms of season, catch limits, and use of catch. A permit is required and the cost of the permit is very much inflated for nonresidents. The message is clear: shrimp baiting is for the locals.

Seafood lingo

The "count" of shrimp refers to how many it takes to make one pound. The count goes down as the growing season progresses and individual shrimp increase in size. Also ask whether the price per pound is for "heads on" or "heads off". A relatively low price per pound may simply reflect the presence of heads.

See also: blue crab, Huntington Beach State Park, flounder, mud minnow, red drum

Southern Flounder

A nice "legal" Flounder.

Flounder fishing in Murrells Inlet.

All eyes on one side

The southern flounder is one of several species of flatfish found in Grand Strand waters. This species is mottled brown above (left side) and light-colored below (right side). Flounders are superbly adapted to life on the bottom. Their bodies are laterally compressed, and during development both eyes move to the left side. This allows the fish to lie on the bottom, partially buried in mud, while at the same time maintaining good visual contact with potential prey items. Coloration and digging ability make these fish virtually invisible when positioned on the bottom.

Getting more flounder

The spawning run in southern flounder begins in fall. Fish older than a year leave the tidal creeks and estuaries and head for offshore spawning sites. When spawning is complete, the adults move back into the estuaries. Larvae hatched in the open waters ride the tidal currents into the estuaries where they eventually settle in nursery habitats. Juvenile flounders feed on invertebrates and fish of the salt marshes but, as they get larger, their diets are almost entirely comprised of fish. Large fish disperse into deeper habitats. The habitat use and spawning patterns of southern flounders are almost identical to two other popular sport fish, the red drum and the spotted seatrout.

Flounder fishing

Fishing for flounders is a popular activity around the Grand Strand. Those with boats go to the tidal creeks of Murrells Inlet. They slow (really slow) troll live mud minnows on rigs that bounce along the bottom. This fishing approach is well suited to the jump-from-the-bottom prey capture tactic of flounder. Some locals are familiar with deep holes in the tidal creeks where flounders are known to congregate at low tide. Flounder are also taken from the piers with shrimp or mud minnows. The current size limit is 12 inches.

Flounder facts

Although most flounders caught in Murrells Inlet are 12 to 15 inches long, the species can get up to 30 inches. Big flounders tend to be associated with deeper waters and can also move into the lower reaches of freshwater rivers. Southern flounders have a sweet, firm flesh that is amenable to many types of cooking methods.

See also: mullet, pinfish, red drum, spot, seatrout

Spot

During spot runs small fishing boats fill Murrells Inlet.

Identifying spot

Short, stocky fish with blunt snouts, spots are related to croakers. Adults are blue/grey with yellow vertical bars. There is a yellow-black spot behind the gill cover. Although a spot can be confused with a pinfish, the mouth of a spot is clearly more geared toward bottom feeding, the upper jaw protruding over the lower jaw. Spots are schooling fish; if you encounter one, you will likely encounter many.

Catching spot: a Myrtle Beach tradition

During the fall, spots run down the coast and also move through estuaries. At these times, hundreds of Grand Strand fishermen pick up their poles and head to the water. Spot fishing is traditional activity that can involve long lines at boat ramps and traffic jams in the parking lots associated with boat ramps. Apparently though, the wait is worth it. Using primarily blood worms as bait and light tackle, fishermen catch large numbers of spots, most of which are less than nine inches long. The fish are cleaned and pan fried.

Food for others

People are not the only ones that actively pursue spots. Striped bass, seatrout, red drum, flounder, and many sea birds feed on them. Juveniles spend most of their lives in shallow estuaries and thus are eaten when these larger game fish enter these habitats. However, adult spots move to offshore areas for spawning and are pursued by many game fish when they make these spawning runs.

Spot trends

Spots are one of the few marine fishes where long-term trends in recreational harvest are steady. Although spots are taken commercially as bycatch in shrimp nets, new methods of small fish exclusion have been successful and the accidental harvest of spots has declined through time.

See also: Atlantic croaker, pinfish, red drum, southern flounder

Tick

Lone star tick   *Deer tick*

Photo used courtesy of the USPHS Centers for Disease Control

A not-so-pleasant wild thing

Ticks are small arthropods more closely related to spiders than to insects. They are parasites that latch on animals and then feed by sucking blood. Anyone venturing into the wild places of the Grand Strand needs to know about these animals because of their potential for spreading a variety of potentially serious diseases. Tick-borne illnesses are not well understood, but with a few precautions the risks can be greatly reduced.

The players

At least five types of ticks are alive and well in South Carolina. Visitors to the Grand Strand will likely encounter the lone star tick and the black-legged or deer tick. The lone star tick transmits Rocky Mountain Spotted Fever and a relatively new disease called Southern Tick-Associated Rash Illness. The black-legged tick transmits Lyme disease. These ticks go through larval, nymph, and adult stages with sizes ranging from very small (size of a freckle or pinhead) to large (size of a pencil eraser). Hosts include small rodents, deer, birds, and humans. Pathogens are present in all stages of tick development.

Understand and avoid

Ticks are superbly adapted for latching on to a host organism. They position themselves on the blades of tall grass or on the outer leaves of shrubs. Any motion elicits a grasping response. Thus as you brush past the vegetation the tick is transferred to your clothing. Most wild habitats around the Grand Strand, with the exception of salt marsh, support ticks and their hosts. If you venture into tick areas, follow these precautions. Wear knee-length rubber boots. These are not easily snagged by ticks. Wear light-colored clothing so that ticks can be spotted and removed. Wear white nylon socks that can be pulled tightly over pant legs. This keeps ticks that fall into your boots from crawling up inside your pants. Spray your clothing, especially in the leg area, with insect repellents. Wear a hat to keep ticks from snagging on your hair.

When the hike is over

After enjoying nature, it is smart to conduct a full body search for ticks. Pay careful attention to the head, armpits, and groin area. Attached ticks should be removed with a pair of tweezers. Grab the tick as close to the skin as possible and pull with steady force. Do not squeeze the tick body as this could release fluids. Apply antiseptic to the bite area and make a note of position and date. Relax and understand that only a small percentage of ticks carry pathogens and that transmission of the pathogen often requires the tick to be attached for at least a day. However, if a rash develops near the bite or if you experience flu-like symptoms after a bite, consult a doctor.

See also: flies, mosquito

White Ibis

Seems like Florida

The white ibis is a long-necked, white wading bird that flies and forages in small flocks. It is instantly recognized by the long, curved pink bill, bare pink face, and pink legs. Although the species is primarily an inhabitant of shallow salt marshes and freshwater wetlands, it is often observed in Grand Strand housing developments. Here, small flocks either roost on the roofs of houses or peck their way through yards. The presence of these birds adds a distinct sense of Florida to the area.

Ibis eats

White ibises eat primarily crabs or crayfish. However, their foraging in yards suggests that they may occasionally dine on worms or grubs. This bird is extremely opportunistic and will feed on those items made vulnerable by dropping water levels. White ibises pursue fish trapped in small pools. They probe the mud with their long bills in search of hidden crayfish. Some fishermen use the ibises as indicators of places where red drum will be feeding when the tide moves back into a salt marsh.

Ibis eggs

As with many wading birds found along the Grand Strand, white ibises nest in groups. Important white ibis nesting sites are scattered along the South Carolina coast but are more likely to occur in freshwater areas where there are extensive shallows. Nests are constructed in small trees and bushes. Stable nests are a limiting resource; females will often lay eggs in the nests of other females.

Ibis history

In the late 1800's white ibises were widely hunted for their feathers, which were then sold as adornments to hats and other types of clothing. Market hunters nearly drove the species to extinction by shooting birds when they congregated in rookeries. With the passing of the Migratory Bird Treaty Act in 1918, market hunting was eliminated and white ibis populations began a long road to recovery. More recently, white ibis populations in South Carolina are relatively stable although, in Florida, water pollution and development are contributing to declining numbers.

See also: fiddler crab, great blue heron, great egret, Huntington Beach State Park

Willet

Photos courtesy of Dr. Reginald Daves

The willet is the largest sandpiper seen commonly on the Grand Strand.   *The distinctive broad white wing stripe marks the willet when it flies.*

Our largest sandpiper

Although the different sandpipers are notoriously hard to identify, the willet is an exception. It is a relatively large shore bird standing about 15 inches tall. At rest the coloration is drab brown and gray but, in flight, the willet exposes an exceptional black- and-white wing pattern. Other distinguishing traits include a long bill and blue legs. Around the Grand Strand, willets are frequently seen on the beach and in salt marshes. They scurry in the surf zone and fly as a group down the beach as beach walkers disturb their hunting.

Getting more willets

Willets are one of the few shore birds living along the Grand Strand that nest on sand dunes and the upper parts of beaches. Nests are located on dry ground or in clumps of grasses and shrubs. Like Canada geese, willets actively defend their nests. Defense actions involve flying around intruders while making loud sounds. After the eggs hatch, families of willets hunt insects and small crustaceans in the marshes until the young are large enough to hunt on the beach. On the beach willets eat coquina clams, worms, and small fish.

Hunted for the market

In the early 1900's willets were driven nearly to extinction by market hunters. However, in contrast to egrets and herons killed for their feathers, willets were hunted for their meat and for their eggs. When market hunting was banned, willets made a rapid recovery and populations are still on the increase.

See also: great egret, great blue heron, sanderling

Wood Duck

The male wood duck is ornate.

Wood duck hens are plainer than their mates, but have a conspicuous white eye ring.

A local resident

Although wood ducks are migratory waterfowl in most parts of the U.S., Grand Strand wood ducks are year-around residents. They are distinct in being the only migratory duck that lives and reproduces in the Grand Strand. The bird's persistent ties to the region can be traced to the abundance of forested swamps. Indeed, most trips into the swamps will reveal numerous pairs of wood ducks flushing from the forest edge. The ornate males are recognized by their purple-blue crested heads decorated with white stripes. The chest is chestnut brown and bordered with a white stripe. Females are gray with white stripes across the eyes.

Tree duck

Wood ducks, as the name indicates, associate with trees in various ways. They are the only common North American duck that regularly perches in trees. Adults consume acorns and maple seeds. They build their nests in tree cavities. Such cavities tend to be found in old, large trees when limbs break off or when woodpeckers have been working. When appropriate nesting sites exist, wood ducks have the abilities to produce several broods of chicks each year. This is particularly true in South Carolina where the reproductive season is long.

Back from the brink

In the early 1900's wood ducks across North America were nearly driven to extinction by market hunting and by logging the old trees that provided nest cavities. However, since the 1960's wood ducks made a dramatic comeback. Part of this can be traced to better protection of forested wetlands. Another part is likely associated with widespread placement of artificial nest boxes. The boxes are made of wood and they have a cone-shaped piece of metal at the bottom that stops nest predation by raccoons and snakes. When placed on poles near water, the nest boxes are readily used. Several such nest boxes can seen at the forest edge across from the Conway Riverwalk and around Lake Busbee.

Ducklings in danger

Because many wood duck chicks come tumbling out of the nest cavities each year, many chick predators wait in the waters. Turtles, largemouth bass, bowfin, raccoons, and other animals take a toll on the chicks as they move through shallow waters in search of invertebrates. However, once the chicks get large enough to perch on branches, life is somewhat safer.

See also: bowfin, freshwater wetland, largemouth bass, yellow-bellied slider

Yellow-Bellied Slider Turtle

Young sliders possess clearly marked shells and a yellow patch near the eyes.

Sun tan turtle

The yellow-bellied slider turtle, or more simply the "slider," is the most commonly observed pond turtle around the Grand Strand. On sunny days, these turtles emerge from the water to bask in the sun. Logs are favorite basking substrates, but culverts and small islands are also used. If sunning sites are limited and sliders are abundant, they pile on top of each other. If approached, the whole group quickly drops in the water. Adult sliders are usually about 8 inches long. They are recognized by the yellow patch behind the eyes. Sliders prefer sluggish bodies of water with an abundance of vegetation, basking sites, and depths to at least 6 feet.

Getting more sliders

Female sliders excavate nests close to the water during spring. Eggs laid in spring will hatch in summer; the young remain in the nest until the following spring. When they emerge from the nest, young sliders are eaten by wading birds, snapping turtles, and raccoons. Baby sliders hide from these predators in the dense aquatic vegetation.

Sliders on the move

When new ponds are constructed, sliders are one of the first reptiles to take up residence. Although sliders are generally aquatic, they can come out of the water and migrate over relatively long distances. Migration occurs along streams but may also occur over land. Whole populations may move when a pond dries up or becomes short on food.

Bobber spotters

Fishermen using live bait consider sliders a great nuisance. Sliders learn quickly to associate the brightly-colored fishing bobber with an easy meal. As soon as a bobber lands in the water all the sliders in the vicinity immediately swim toward it and then wrestle for the bait. If a slider is hooked or snagged, slowly reel it in and then firmly grab the turtle around the neck, using pliers to quickly remove the hook. Sliders will bite, so use caution.

See also: American alligator, eastern cottonmouth, freshwater wetland, loggerhead sea turtle

Plants of the Grand Strand

Bald cypress

Bald cypress knees along the Waccamaw River. (right) Bald cypress leaves.

What is it?

Bald cypress is a tree commonly found growing in swamps and inundated areas along the Grand Strand. It has several features that make it easy to identify. Leaves are needle-like and they are shed in winter. Thus bald cypress is one of the few deciduous conifers. When growing in water, bald cypress develops a wide flared base with much buttressing. Cypress knees, upward projections from the lateral roots, can be seen around individual trees and provide improved stability in wet soils. Most bald cypress trees are laden with Spanish moss, giving cypress swamps a closed and dark appearance.

Why did they cut all the cypress trees?

Swamps along the Grand Strand once supported massive forests of bald cypress. In the 1700's some stands were cleared to make rice fields. By the 1900's most of the old-growth forests were cut and the logs were put to many uses. The most important characteristic of large cypress logs is resistance to rot. This is due to the presence of an oil that waterproofs the wood. Indeed, cypress was once used for the construction of boats, shingles, and barrels. The water control structures used to divert water in the rice fields were made from bald cypress and some of these persist today. However, rot resistance is a characteristic that only emerges in large, old trees. Smaller trees today are used for the construction of specialty furniture.

When cypress stems are invaded by a certain species of fungus, the result is a type of wood called pecky cypress. Pecky cypress, filled with holes, makes a unique decorative building material where resistance to water is not important.

Bald cypress as a living community

Bald cypress trees support and nourish a large variety of other organisms. The seeds are eaten by many animals. Veteran trees at the edges of swamps are favorite nesting and perching sites of osprey. Prothonotary warblers build nests in rotting cypress knees. Catfish and bowfin seek refuge in the buttresses. Most importantly, many plants that grow in swamps can only establish on the raised areas formed by cypress bases and knees.

Getting new bald cypress trees

The seeds of bald cypress float with the water current. However, they will not germinate in areas of standing water. Thus, new stands of bald cypress must originate on moist land surfaces where water is temporarily absent. Although bald cypress is a tree of the swamps, it is clear that swamps must dry out at some point in order to get new trees established.

Where can I see them?

Just about any low-lying are a with standing or flowing fresh water will support some bald cypress. However, a particularly good view of a bald cypress stand is from the Conway Riverwalk. Here the river is under tidal influence. The dark areas at the bases of the trees indicate the water level at high tide.

See also: bowfin, Conway Riverwalk, freshwater wetland, osprey, Waccamaw National Wildlife Refuge

Bay Trees

Sweetbay is a member of the Magnolia family. (above)
Red Bay leaves and stems. (top right)
A Loblolly bay leaf. (bottom right)

A trio of bay trees

Three species of bay trees are common in the Grand Strand area. All are evergreens with smooth, leathery leaves. Sweet bay resembles the southern magnolia although it is smaller, the undersides of the leaves are whitish, and the white flowers are not as showy. Loblolly bay is a shrub or tree that occurs primarily in wet forests. The leaves have shallow teeth along the edges and are often ragged due to insect damage. Red bay is also found in wet forests. The leaves lack teeth and have a pleasant smell when crushed. They also often carry small bumps (galls) caused by a plant louse. Of these three bay trees, sweet bay is most frequently planted around the home because of its tolerance of many soil conditions and its floral display.

Bay trees and depressions

The Grand Strand landscape is marked by small variations in topography. While driving down roads you experience this as a series of low ridges and depressions. Notice how the understory of pine forests changes. Relatively open pine stands on the ridges turn to relatively dense and closed stands in depressions. Red bay, sweet bay and loblolly bay are good indicators of depressions. These trees can in some places form an almost impenetrable layer in the understory of pine forests. Carolina bays, depressional wetlands that occur in the Grand Strand area, are named after the bay trees that grow there.

The value of evergreens

Evergreen trees such as bays are well-suited to the infertile soils that occur in the Grand Strand region. Evergreen leaves are costly for the plant to make, but they are retained on the tree for long periods of time. Thus, the trees use relatively fewer soil nutrients and can also capture the sun's energy during winter.

Uses of bay trees

Seeds of these trees are consumed by many birds. Deer feed heavily on the foliage. The leaves of red bay are widely used as a spice, their taste resembling that of commercially available bay leaves that come from a different plant species.

See also: Carolina bay, Lewis Ocean Bay Heritage Preserve, pine, wax-myrtle

Common reed

63

Common reed is an introduced plant.

What is it?

Common reed is a tall (5-15 feet high), perennial grass that forms large colonies by production of fast-growing underground or creeping structures (rhizomes). It is widely distributed around the world although it is a relatively new addition to wetland habitats along the Grand Strand. Common reed is readily observed in roadside ditches, brackish marshes, at the edges of shallow ponds, and in areas where dredged materials have been dumped. The species is easily identified by the purplish-brown plumes (flowers) at the tips of the stems.

Common reed: the invader

Common reed was introduced to South Carolina wetlands as a result of dredging operations associated with the Intracoastal Waterway. Pieces of rhizomes were scattered among the dredged material and then planted in spoil disposal sites. Seeds and rhizomes were further dispersed by water currents. Common reed is an aggressive and highly productive species that can dominate certain types of areas. Specifically, it thrives in brackish marshes where saltwater mixes with freshwater or where inputs of nutrients such as nitrogen are elevated. Stands of common reed are so thick that few other plants can survive. Common reed supports a relatively depauperate animal community. Resource managers attempt to eradicate the plant, but this is often a hopeless endeavor.

Common reed: an indicator

Invasive plants such as common reed may indicate specific types of changes in ecological systems. More specifically, common reed shows us where soils have been disturbed or where pollution may be occurring. Thus, it is important to understand the distribution and importance of common reed around the Grand Strand.

Where can I see it?

An extensive stand of common reed can be viewed from the Winyah Bay Fishing and Observation Pier. Here the brackish marshes that once supported rice fields have been almost completely invaded. No one knows for sure how this invasion has affected ecological processes in the area, but some studies are now underway.

See also: smooth cordgrass, freshwater wetland, salt marsh, Winyah Bay Fishing and Observation Pier

Firewheel

The firewheel is a colorful dune flower. (above)
Close up of the daisy-like flower of the firewheel. (right)

What is it?

Firewheel is a plant commonly found growing on the protected backsides of sand dunes and in sand along parking lots at the beach. The name is derived from the flowers that are bright red with yellow tips. Plants can grow up to 2 feet tall, however those growing at the beach are typically shorter and are found in either tight clumps or lying flat along the ground. Flowering begins in early summer and continues until fall. In some places, firewheel forms a continuous blanket of flowers that attracts both photographers and flower collectors. It is extremely tolerant of drought and thus can be found in sandy sites where other plants cannot grow. In colder climates the plant functions as an annual. However, in the southeast it may live for several years

Where did it come from?

Botanists think that firewheel is native to the western United States. This is likely a species that was carried east by gardeners. The plant then escaped and has spread throughout eastern states. Firewheel is a plant that has long attracted the attention of plant breeders. A trip to the local plant store will reveal many varieties of firewheel (also named Gaillardia or blanket flower) that have been developed for their unique forms and flower colors.

Can I take it home?

Provided that you are not in a state park or protected area, seeds of firewheel can be collected and transported. The white, ripe seeds are produced in round clusters and are typically available throughout the summer. Seeds sown in your garden during late summer and fall will germinate and produce flowers during the following year. The flowers are well-suited for cutting and drying. However, don't expect plants to persist in the garden beyond a year.

Holding on

Although firewheel is not considered a native species of the sand dune habitat, it likely serves an important role in stabilizing sand dunes. It is one of the few species that can tolerate mild trampling by humans. Thus, firewheels should be protected when possible. There is another reason why one should not venture near patches of firewheel. It grows in association with the dune sandbur, a plant that can inflict serious pain on barefoot beachgoers.

See also: Myrtle Beach State Park, sandbur, sea-oats, sea rocket, yaupon

Glasswort

Glasswort grows where salts accumulate in the salt marsh. (above)
The thick stem of glasswort stores water. (inset)

What is it?
Glasswort, a small plant with finger-like, jointed stems, forms low creeping mats on salt flats. Leaves are represented by scales. Stems are initially green but turn red with age. The plant is a halophyte, a species that can tolerate very high salt concentrations.

Why are salt flats salty?
In elevated areas of salt marshes far from the tidal creeks, inundation occurs only at extremely high tides. Thus salt accumulates due to the absence of flushing. Furthermore, small depressions trap the water and evaporation leads to salt deposits. In these areas few plants can survive except for glasswort. Some salt flats are so salty that only bare ground is present.

How does glasswort tolerate the salt?
Glasswort has thick, fleshy stems. The fleshy tissue allows for storage of relatively large amounts of water. This is important, as it is difficult for glasswort to absorb water from the salty substrate. Furthermore, glasswort accumulates excess salts in the tips of the stems. These tips break off at the joints and thus salt is eliminated from the plant. When you walk through a stand of glasswort the stems break like glass.

Tasting the tips
The tender newly produced stems of glasswort make a tasty albeit salty snack. Some people even make salads and pickles from them.

Where can I find them?
Glassworts are found in the high marsh in places where all other vegetation has been eliminated. Find bare areas, and glasswort will be nearby.

See also: smooth cordgrass, Huntington Beach State Park, salt marsh, sea rocket

Live Oak

Majestic live oaks line the streets of Conway. (above)
Live oaks this large may be more than 150 years old. (top right)
Live oak leaves and acorns. (right)

The tree and its habitat

There is perhaps no better known sign of the "old south" than the majestic live oak with its low sweeping branches covered with Spanish-moss. This evergreen oak with furrowed bark is a species that grows naturally along the coast. When close to the beach, it tolerates salt spray but may take on a stunted form, thus contributing to the maritime forest. When not inhibited by salt spray and when given plenty of space, live oaks grow large and live for many years. Some champion live oaks are nearly 1500 years old. Their trunks approach 6 feet in diameter.

Uses and abuses

Many live oaks were historically cut and used for construction purposes. The wood is extremely dense. The curved branches were particularly suited for making the supporting ribs of ships. In 1799 public lands were pre-served solely to maintain live oaks for ship-building purposes. Live oaks were also planted along the lanes leading up to many southern plantations. These trees, once they reached adult size, created the arch effect so important in the plantation landscape. The value of live oak as a shade tree can be readily appreciated with a visit to the picnic area at Myrtle Beach State Park.

Live oaks of Conway

The City of Conway recognized that live oaks make an important contribution to the beauty and appeal of the older neighborhoods. A brochure, The Oaks of Conway, is available at the Chamber of Commerce. Many of the biggest trees along the streets of Conway were inventoried, measured and mapped. Ordinances were passed to protect these Landmark Trees within city limits. Development projects must work around and protect all live oaks greater than 8 inches in diameter. A drive through Conway will show several places where roads were built around live oak trees.

Acorns for all

Live oak trees produce large quantities of acorns, which serve as an important source of food for squirrels, bears, turkeys, and deer. Recent studies conducted after Hurricane Hugo suggest that live oak is also extremely resistant to wind damage. Thus the tree represents a stable source of food that likely continues to produce while other species are recovering from wind damage.

See also: Conway Riverwalk, Myrtle Beach State Park, pine, Spanish-moss

Palmetto

Dwarf palmetto grow in swamps and dense maritime forests.

A palm at every corner

Of the many wild things that leave lasting impressions, the palms of the Grand Strand are perhaps most influential. Live oaks draped with Spanish moss frame the inland old south, but it is palms that characterize the beach. Visitors to the Grand Strand will see many types of palms, some native and some not. Two species are particularly important in the history and ecology of the region.

The one that acts like a tree

Cabbage palmetto is an evergreen tree with an unbranched trunk that grows to about 50 feet tall. The blades of the leaves have whitish string-like filaments, and the flowering stems have many flowers. The trunks of young cabbage palmettos are covered with tough leaf bases, but in older trees these fall off and the trunks are relatively smooth. Cabbage palmettos are widely used in landscape plantings and are tolerant of some salt spray. The flexible trunks also allow them to withstand the rigors of hurricanes.

The Cabbage palmetto is South Carolina's state tree.

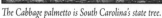

The one that acts like a shrub

Dwarf palmetto may get up to 20 feet high but is usually a shrub. It lacks the thread-like filaments on the leaves and is typically found growing in the understory of wet forests. It is recognized by the large fan-shaped leaves. Good specimens of dwarf palmetto can be found in the forest at Myrtle Beach State Park and along the Crabtree Recreation Trail.

The South Carolina state symbol

The cabbage palmetto is the state symbol of South Carolina. Promoters of the state have put the image of the plant on everything imaginable. Adoption of this plant as the official symbol can be traced to the Revolutionary War. A small fort on Charleston Harbor was constructed of cabbage palmetto logs. The force of cannonballs fired by the British was admirably absorbed by the logs and thus the invaders were repelled. Cabbage palmetto represents strength.

A smorgasbord of palms

Both cabbage palmetto and dwarf palmetto are used by many types of animals. The flowers attract a large variety of pollinators. The fruits are eaten by birds and mammals. And the dead leaves provide habitat for a variety of ground-dwelling reptiles. Cabbage palmettos produce a terminal bud that can be cooked and eaten by people. Extremely large cockroaches known as palmetto bugs may be found on palmettos, but more likely will be found scurrying across the bedroom floor.

See also: Crabtree Recreation Trail, Myrtle Beach State Park, Sandy Island

Peat Moss

Tiny moss plants create peat.

What is it?

Peat moss - also known as sphagnum moss - is a small plant that rarely exceeds 3 inches in height. However, individual plants grow in dense stands that may in some areas completely cover the ground. There are many different species of peat moss that range in color from green to bright red. Different species also have slightly different habitat requirements. Some grow in flooded areas; others can tolerate drier soil.

Where does it grow?

Peat moss thrives on peaty or sandy soils that are low in nutrients. Along the Grand Strand peat moss is found associated with Carolina Bays where it may form extensive carpets. It also forms small mounds at the edges of ponds and ditches. When it grows along ditches, one can almost be certain that the ditch cut across some portion of a previously existing Carolina Bay.

What does it do?

Peat moss growth occurs at the upper ends of individual stems. Previous growth is buried by new growth. The dead, buried tissue of peat moss (peat) then becomes an important substrate in wetland systems. Peat has many unique characteristics that shape the function of wetlands along the Grand Strand. Most importantly, peat absorbs and holds large quantities of water, thus making wetlands function as large sponges. Peat is a good soil conditioner; it can be purchased in large bags at garden stores. Commercially available peat has been mined from northern bogs where peat accumulations are much deeper than in South Carolina.

The Indians and peat moss

Indians used peat moss for many purposes. With natural antibiotic properties, it made a good wound dressing. Children's pants were lined with peat moss to make the first disposable but absorbent diapers.

See also: Carolina Bay, freshwater wetland, Lewis Ocean Bay Heritage Preserve, pine, Venus' fly trap

Pickerel Weed

Pickerel weed is a common aquatic flowering plant. (above)
The flowers of pikerel weed are purplish-blue. (inset)

What is it?

Pickerel weed is a perennial wetland plant with large heart-shaped leaves. It roots at the edges of ponds, ditches, and sloughs where it may form colonies. The plants grow 3 to 5 feet tall. The purplish-blue flowers are produced throughout the growing season on spikes that may project above the leaves. This is one of the Grand Strand's most attractive wetland plants.

In the backyard pond

Water gardeners covet this plant because of its shiny leaves and showy flowers. It is easy to propagate. Simply obtain some stems with sections of attached rhizomes and plant these either in submerged pots or directly in soil at the pond edge. The plant grows best in water about 12 inches deep. In some parts of the country pickerel weed has been identified as invasive due to rapid growth. However, along the Grand Strand it remains under control perhaps due to the large number of animals that feed on it.

A breath of air for wetlands

Pickerel weed as well as many other emergent wetland plants has the ability to move oxygen from the leaves through the stem and down into the roots. The oxygen is important for maintaining the root systems, but it also leaks out of the roots and is made available to other organisms. Bacteria living close to the roots of pickerel weed are stimulated by this oxygen loss. Thus pickerel weed is important for keeping wetlands well aerated. Artificial wetlands constructed for treating wastewater are often planted with pickerel weed.

A wetland community

Many animals live on and around pickerel weed. The name of the plant apparently comes from the fact that pickerel hide among the stems. Dragonflies deposit eggs on the stems. Birds consume the seeds. Muskrats and beavers feed on the rhizomes and stems.

See also: freshwater wetland, Myrtle Beach State Park, storm water detention pond, water-hyacinth

Pine

Longleaf pine in its grass stage.

Long leaf pines have the largest needles and cones.

Loblolly pine

Pond pine cones

Which ones will you see?

Along the Grand Strand pine trees can be seen in most forested areas. These are recognized as trees with long needles and persistent cones. Three species are common: loblolly pine, longleaf pine, and pond pine. Loblolly pine is perhaps the most widely distributed. It has 6-inch leaves in clusters of threes. Longleaf pine has 10-inch leaves in clusters of threes. Pond pine also has 6-inch leaves in clusters of threes but the cones are small, usually less than 4 inches long.

Longleaf pine of the past

Early settlers in South Carolina encountered large areas of longleaf pine growing in relatively open park-like settings (savannas). The longleaf pine ecosystem was fire maintained. Many think that Indians set frequent fires in order to encourage game and to make travel less difficult. With settlement came various impacts. Specifically, longleaf pine was an important source of turpentine and pine resin. This fueled the South Carolina economy from the early 1700's to mid 1800's. From the late 1800's to the early 1900's the last remaining old growth longleaf pine stands were cut for timber.

Loblolly: the pine of the future

With the elimination of longleaf pine and the reduced frequency of fire, longleaf pine areas were replaced by loblolly pines. Loblolly is a fast-growing species that can reproduce and grow well on a wide range of sites, including relatively wet bottomlands. In 20 years stems may reach 10 inches in diameter. It is now considered the most commercially important tree in the southeast. Loblolly pines around the Grand Strand grow mixed with oaks and other broadleaf trees. Loblolly pines are also cultivated in large pine plantations by the timber companies.

Carolina Bays and pond pines

Pond pines grow in wet areas. Specifically, they are found in depressional wetlands known as Carolina Bays. The seed cones remain closed until scorched by fires. Then the cones open and seeds are released. This adaptation assures that seeds fall on relatively open soils.

See also: Carolina Bay, Lewis Ocean Bay Heritage Preserve, Sandy Island, switchcane

Pitcher Plant

Yellow trumpet pitcher plants at Lewis Ocean Bay Heritage Preserve. (above)
The flower of the yellow trumpet pitcher plant (inset)

The plant that collects insects

Pitcher plants are the most prominent carnivorous plants found along the Grand Strand. They capture insects in funnel-shaped leaves, and thus gain some nutrients when the insects are digested. Although several species of pitcher plants occur in the southeast, the most common one in our area is the yellow trumpet pitcher plant. It produces tall, narrow pitchers up to 3 feet tall and large flowers with yellow petals. Each pitcher has a prominent lid. Pitcher plants grow at the edges of Carolina bays and also along ditches that have been dug through what once was a Carolina bay. They are typically found in association with other carnivorous plants such as Venus' fly traps and sundews.

The trap as a trap

Pitcher plants attract insects to the mouth of the pitcher by various mechanisms. In some cases nectar is produced while in other cases color patterns serve as the attractant. Once insects enter the opening of the trap they slip into the bottom of the pitcher and eventually die. Digestive juices released by the plant then reduce the insects to a usable form. Pitchers are so efficient at insect capture that they may bend with the accumulated weight of dead insects.

The trap as a habitat

All pitcher plants create a unique environment inside their pitchers. In some cases rainwater accumulates in pitchers thus forming micro-ponds. In other cases, the inside of the pitcher is simply moist and is filled with decomposing insects. This habitat is not deadly for all organisms. Indeed, many invertebrates live inside the pitchers where they find both a constant source of food and suitable habitat. When pitcher plants are eliminated due to habitat destruction, we lose these interesting plants and the organisms that they support.

Threats to pitchers

Throughout the Grand Strand, carnivorous plants such as pitcher plants and Venus' fly traps are rapidly vanishing primarily as a result of habitat destruction. Efforts are underway to identify populations of these plants. When destruction is inevitable, plants are moved to safer locations. One safe haven for carnivorous plants is Lewis Ocean Bay Heritage Preserve. A drive through this area will reveal thousands of yellow trumpet pitcher plants growing along the drainage ditches.

See also: Carolina bay, freshwater wetland, Lewis Ocean Bay Heritage Preserve, Venus' fly trap

Poison Ivy

Leaves in three, let it be.

A vine to avoid

Poison ivy is a widespread vine that forms tangled thickets in several Grand Strand habitats. This species is easy to identify. Look for a woody vine that may climb on other plants and trees, or creep across the ground. The woody stems are often covered with root-like projections that allow the plant grab on to other objects. It produces alternate leaves that are divided into three distinct leaflets. Each leaflet actually looks like a whole leaf. The leaflets are pointed at the ends and dark, shiny green on the top; the central leaflet is long stalked and clusters of ivory fruits occur along the stems. Most parts of the poison ivy plant produce an oil called urushiol. This oil causes an allergic reaction in many people. The reaction involves an itchy rash and development of blisters.

Where it grows

Because of its growth characteristics, poison ivy is often found in the very same places where humans travel. It thrives when any disturbance creates an opening in the existing vegetation. Such openings have greater light availability and poison ivy responds by growing faster and by producing more shoots. Birds that eat the fruits and disperse the seeds of poison ivy are also attracted to openings. Good examples of such openings are trails and roads. Thus we often find dense stands of poison ivy at the edges of trails and roads. For example, at Lewis Ocean Bay Heritage Preserve poison ivy grows along most of the roads. It is relatively rare once you venture off of the roads.

Taking out the itch

Poison ivy is not typically a problem for hikers as long as they avoid contact with the plant by wearing long pants and boots. Others may get contact by clearing brush in winter (the oil is found in the stems and roots), by burning brush (the oil can be transmitted in smoke), or by touching objects that have been in poison ivy patches (pets and clothing can transmit the oil). If you make contact with poison ivy, wash the skin with plenty of soap and water or apply lots of rubbing alcohol.

Wax myrtle or poison ivy?

There is only one other common Grand Strand plant that might be confused with poison ivy. Wax myrtle also produces clusters of light-colored fruits. However, the leaves of wax myrtle are not divided into three leaflets and wax myrtle does not grow as a vine.

See also: Lewis Ocean Bay Heritage Preserve, sandbur, wax-myrtle, yaupon

Sandbur

Sandburs often grow in disturbed areas near sand dunes. (above)
Fruits of the sandbur are superbly adapted to hitching a ride on animals. (inset)

The beach plant to avoid
There are several species of sandbur that occur in the Grand Strand region. Dune sandbur is an annual grass often found growing along boardwalks leading to the beaches. Common sandbur is a creeping annual grass found in trampled areas near parking lots. Both plants produce burs with sharp spines that will stick in unprotected legs and feet. Sandburs will often be found growing in close association with firewheel.

Traveling from beach to beach
Sandburs are most prominent in heavily used beach areas. There are two reasons for this. First, sandburs grow in disturbed sands where competition from other plants is low. Heavily used beach areas have a lot of disturbed sand. Second, the burs get stuck in all types of beach equipment such as umbrellas, bags, and towels. As the equipment is taken from beach to beach, more seeds get brought into areas with more beach traffic.

Stick to the walkways
Boardwalks and sidewalks leading to the beach are in place to protect dune vegetation from trampling. Often, the urge to get on the beach causes people to cut corners. However, the presence of sandburs is one very good reason why you should suppress this urge. Sandburs will even penetrate the bottom of some beach sandals, so stick to the walkways.

An unpleasant plant surprise
If you hiked through a back dune area on your way to the beach, it is always a good idea to inspect beach towels before you use them. Sandburs seem almost able to leap onto beach towels where they wait for the back sides of unsuspecting sunbathers.

See also: firewheel, sea-oats, sea rocket, smooth cordgrass

Sea Oats

Sea oats help stabilize sand dunes. (above)
Sea oats seedhead. (inset)

The southern grass of the beaches

Sea oats is the major perennial grass that thrives on sand dunes in the Grand Strand area. It has a tuft of leaves near the sand surface and also produces single leaves along the 4-8 foot high stems. The name "sea oats" was given because the flowers and seeds resemble those of cultivated oats. Sea oats, like many common Grand Strand plants, produces an extensive rhizome system. These long under ground stems are often exposed when sand is eroded from a dune system.

Catching sand

Sea oats builds and stabilizes sand dunes. For this reason, it is protected by law and areas where sea oats grows are off-limits to people. The tuft of leaves near the sand slows down the wind and thus wind-blown sand is deposited on the back sides of individual plants. In response to sand accumulation, sea oats sends rhizomes and roots into the growing dune thus stabilizing the system. Clumps of sea oats also trap seeds of other plants and make the environment more favorable for these species to establish. Sea oats is tolerant of salt spray and drought. Thus it is superbly suited to the dune environment.

Making dunes

In some parts of the country sea oats are planted in dune systems as a way of speeding up the stabilization process. Seeds are collected in the wild and germinated in greenhouses. The individual plants are then grown in pots. When the plants reach critical size they are planted into bare dunes. These restored dunes are often recognized by the regular pattern of the plants. Dunes formed naturally have a great variety of sizes and shapes. Dunes formed by planting are more uniform.

Dune food

Sea oats provides food for the few animal species that live on or near dunes. Mice and birds eat the seeds. Ghost crabs frequently pile the seeds at the openings of their burrows. It is, however, unknown whether or not they eat these seeds.

See also: firewheel, sand dunes, sandbur, yaupon

Sea Rocket

Sea rocket on a foredune. (above)
The sea rocket flower (inset)

What is it?

Sea rocket is an annual plant related to broccoli and cauliflower. It grows at the upper edge of beaches along the Grand Strand. Indeed, it is the only plant that commonly lives on the beach beyond the foredune area. It has fleshy stems and thick bluntly toothed leaves that hold large quantities of water. The light pink flowers have four petals and the abundant seed pods resemble small rockets. The seed pods are produced at the ends of the stems.

How does it get there?

The seeds and seed pods of sea rocket float. Thus the seeds are dispersed by water. Sea rockets are found growing on the beach where debris (wrack) was previously deposited by high tides. The debris buries the seeds and also provides a suitable environment for germination. Sea rockets are some of the first plants to colonize new islands presumably because of seeds floating in the ocean currents.

What about that name?

On first inspection, one concludes that the name "sea rocket" comes from the rocket-like shape of the seed pod. However, this is not the case. Leaves and seed pods of sea rockets have been consumed by people for many years. The plant has a tangy taste that some say resembles that of horseradish, but chemicals in the tissue also cause gas. Release of this gas in the form of belching was at one time associated with the word rocket. You may eat the plant, but be prepared for the unpleasant side effects.

See also: fiddler crab, Huntington Beach State Park, seaweed, sea-oats

Seaweed

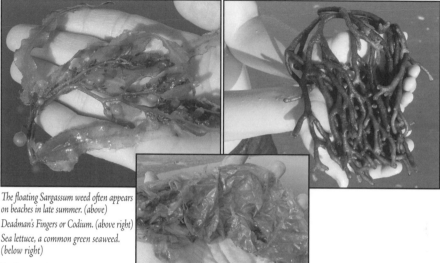

The floating Sargassum weed often appears on beaches in late summer. (above)

Deadman's Fingers or Codium. (above right)

Sea lettuce, a common green seaweed. (below right)

Botany 101

Seaweeds or marine algae comprise a fascinating group of plants with complex life cycles. The seaweed experts (called phycologists) recognize three types of seaweeds: green algae, brown algae, and red algae. This distinction is based on the presence or absence of various pigments and thus the color of the plants. Green algae tend to be found in shallow waters; brown algae and red algae grow at greater depths. However, some algae don't follow this general rule. Seaweeds can assume a variety of shapes ranging from microscopic threads, to finger-like projections, to thin sheets. All of them use the sun's energy to drive the production of sugars.

Gulfweed comes to the beach

Visitors to Grand Strand beaches often have their beach experience marred by the presence of a brown algae known as Sargassum or gulfweed. Gulfweed is recognized by the brown, ribbon-like blades dotted with gas-filled bulbs. Gulfweed grows in large rafts that float at the surface of warm Gulf Stream waters. Storms frequently bring gulfweed to the Grand Strand and waves deposit the plants on the beach in long rows. Dead gulfweed, when it rots, has an unpleasant smell. Thus, many resorts along the beach attempt to remove it with rakes or with heavy equipment. But, before you declare gulfweed a nuisance consider this fact: floating rafts of gulfweed provide habitat for many species of fish. Some fish spend their entire lives in the gulfweed. Gulfweed is so important in the life cycle of mahi mahi that harvest of the plant in offshore areas is regulated.

Sea lettuce and dead man's fingers respond to water quality

Sea lettuce is a green alga found growing on shallow mud flats. The plant appears as bright green, wrinkled sheets of soft paper. Dead man's fingers is an introduced species of green algae that forms spongy, rope-like structures. Both algae are frequently dislodged from the bottom and from mud flats by waves and are washed onto beaches. Both algae grow faster in response to pulses of nutrients such as nitrogen and phosphorus. In polluted waters receiving sewage inputs, they may cover the bottom and smother other types of organisms. Good stands of sea lettuce and other marine algae can be seen growing on the jetty rocks at Huntington Beach State Park.

Algal eats

Seaweeds in general have been used as food (e.g., the red algae used to bind sushi), as a source of food additives (e.g., the thickener carrageenan also derived from red algae), and as various cosmetics and medicines. The same gulfweed that washes onto Grand Strand beaches is used as a treatment for cancer in China. Sea lettuce can be eaten in salads and in soups.

See also: bottlenose dolphin, Huntington Beach State Park, jellyfish, salt marsh

Smooth cordgrass or Spartina is the dominant plant in salt marshes where it helps stabilize sediments.

What is it?

Salt marshes along the Grand Strand are dominated by smooth cordgrass. This is a thick, perennial grass that produces an extensive underground rhizome/root system. Plants may get up to 8 feet high but 4 feet is more common in our area. In summers the leaves are blue-green, but in winter these turn golden yellow. At sunset the leaves of smooth cordgrass reflect light in ways that invite the efforts of photographers.

What does it do?

Smooth cordgrass is one of the few species that can tolerate daily inundation by salt water. It readily colonizes tidal flats when its seeds float into these sites. More commonly however, established clumps of smooth cordgrass are eroded from the banks of tidal creeks and entire plants are transported by water to new areas. Cordgrass stems with rhizomes attached are often found washed up on the beach. Once smooth cordgrass is established it traps and stabilizes more sediment.

Big ones and little ones

Scientists have identified two types of smooth cordgrass. A tall type grows near the tidal creeks where tidal flushing is most intense. A short type grows at higher elevations where salt accumulates to relatively greater levels. Regardless of size, smooth cordgrass is a key organism of the salt marsh. Periwinkles graze on it. Birds consume the seeds. Muskrats feast on the rhizomes. Banks of dead smooth cordgrass called wrack provide habitat for crabs.

A marsh engineer

Smooth cordgrass stabilizes sediments in marshes by vigorous growth and production of extensive belowground structures. Cordgrass in turn provides habitat and food for other organisms. When a single plant species has dramatic and far-reaching effects on the immediate environment, it is considered an ecological engineer. In the absence of smooth cordgrass, the salt marsh ecosystem would be much different. Indeed, in the absence of smooth cordgrass the salt marsh would not exist.

See also: fiddler crab, glasswort, Huntington Beach State Park, salt marsh periwinkle

Spanish Moss

What is it?

Spanish moss is the grey hair-like plant hanging in masses from the branches of older trees in the Grand Strand area. It is not a true moss, but rather a flowering plant related to the pineapple. It has no roots for uptake of water and nutrients and is thus an epiphyte, a plant that depends on other plants for support. The name "Spanish moss" comes from the French; they thought it resembled the beards of Spanish explorers that preceded them to the New World.

An indicator of air quality

Stems and the small scale-like leaves of Spanish moss absorb nutrients from the rain and from the air. The plants are sensitive indicators of air quality. For example, oak trees located near chimneys will not support growth of Spanish moss. Plants growing in urban areas can actually be used as indicators of various air pollutants. Lush growth of Spanish moss indicates both good air quality and protection from the wind.

Spanish moss lives on many trees, most famously the live oak.

A special type of growth

All plants carry out photosynthesis, a process where light energy is used to make sugars. Spanish moss uses a special type of photosynthesis that is active at night. This conserves water and allows plants to remain wet in a dry environment that is isolated from sources of water in the soil.

A novel building material

The core of the Spanish moss stem is made of a tough fiber. This fiber has been used as a stuffing for seats and mattresses. The plant has also been mixed with clay to form a type of mortar in buildings. The dried stems make an attractive matrix for flower arrangement. Birds commonly use the plants for building nests. In the process of carrying Spanish moss, they also spread it from branch to branch and from tree to tree. Commercial harvest of Spanish moss occurs in some southern states, but this has never been an important part of the South Carolina economy. Many insects, mites, spiders, and lizards live in the clumps of Spanish moss.

See also: Conway Riverwalk, live oak, Myrtle Beach State Park, peat moss,

Switchcane

Introduced bamboos grow in many Grand Strand locations. (above)
Switchcane plants along a wetland. (far right) The rhizome or root system of swtichcane. (inset)

What is it?

Switchcane (a type of grass) represents the only native species of bamboo found in the U.S. Along the Grand Stand, patches of switchcane are commonly seen at the edges of pine forests and in moist bottomlands. In our area, stems of this species do not usually exceed 8 ft in height and are less than one inch in diameter. In other areas, the species achieves greater stature. Switchcane forms colonies or cane brakes by producing a stout underground stem. This stem or rhizome gives rise to new aboveground canes.

Uses and abuses

Switchcane has been used for many purposes for many years. Split-cane mats and baskets were made by the Indians. Cane-back and cane-bottom chairs are still available. Larger canes are cut and used as fishing poles although non-native species serve better in this regard. At one time, cane brakes were extensive particularly in bottomland areas. However, cattle readily consume the young shoots and leaves; under continuous grazing pressure cane brakes eventually are eliminated. Cane brakes also occurred on rich soils converted to agriculture.

A time to flower; a time to die

Switchcane periodically flowers and sets seed. As with many species of bamboo, flowering is sometimes associated with plant death. However, this has not been widely documented and cultivated plants will flower repeatedly. Frequent burning keeps switchcane in a stunted form that inhibits flowering.

The big bamboos

While driving around the Grand Strand, visitors will commonly see patches of very large bamboo growing near houses or on old home sites. These are species that have been imported from China, Japan, or Korea. Non-native bamboos can achieve tree-like proportions. In the native habitat they are used for food (bamboo shoots) and as construction materials. Expensive bamboo fishing rods are made from Tonkin cane, a species that grows in China.

See also: common reed, Lewis Ocean Bay Heritage Preserve, pine

Venus' Fly Trap

The Venus' fly trap catches insects in its "jawlike" leaves. (above)
White flowers of the Venus' fly trap occur on tall stalks, well above the traps. (inset)

I know what they are but.....
Most people are familiar with the Venus' fly trap and its ability to capture and digest insects. Indeed, this species may be one of the most famous of all carnivorous plants. However, few people know that the Venus' fly trap is native to the Grand Strand region. Specifically, it occurs naturally in Horry County and in a small region near Wilmington, North Carolina. The Venus' fly trap has leaves modified into snap traps. These traps close on insects and thus the plant gains much-needed nutrients such as nitrogen.

Where can I see it?
Your best bet for seeing a Venus' fly trap is to visit a botanical garden where bog gardens containing carnivorous plants are maintained. In the Grand Strand region, Venus' fly traps occur in Lewis Ocean Bay Heritage Preserve, but populations are few and far between. The species grows at the edges of Carolina bays where the proper combination of moisture and fire produces the right habitat. It is often found growing among peat moss and the best time to find it is in June when the white flowers are visible.

A rare plant with shrinking habitat
Botanists have long monitored populations of the Venus' fly trap in North Carolina and South Carolina. Outside of nature preserves, habitat destruction is the major cause of declining numbers. Illegal collecting of plants in the wild is also a factor. Because Lewis Ocean Bay Heritage Preserve has such a large amount of potential habitat, research is now underway to propagate new populations of Venus' fly traps. Frequent burning is critical in this effort because, without fire, shrubs form dense thickets and eventually cover up the plants.

From Horry County to the world
The Venus' fly trap is a horticultural novelty and has been distributed throughout the world. Many varieties differing in trap shape and color have been selected by growers. Commercial production of the Venus' fly trap now occurs through tissue culture, thus eliminating the need for further plant collection in the wild. If you are lucky enough to see a Venus' fly trap do not disturb it or its immediate habitat.

See also: Bay tree, Carolina bay, Lewis Ocean Bay Heritage Preserve, peat moss

Water Hyacinth

Water hyacinths, lovely, but a nuisance.

A lovely but noxious plant

Water hyacinth is a floating aquatic plant that in some parts of the U.S. causes many ecological problems. Individual plants consist of a whorl of leaves (a rosette). Each oval-shaped leaf blade (about 4 inches wide) is attached to an air-filled petiole (stem). The petioles are buoyant and allow the plant to float freely. Roots and rhizomes at the base of the plant extend down into the water. Showy blue flowers are produced on separate stems. Water hyacinth grows in ditches and ponds. It is also well-established in the Waccamaw River where one can readily find stranded plants deposited on the banks by rising waters.

The invasion

Water hyacinth, native to tropical South America, was introduced to the U.S. in the late 1800's. It is now considered a weed in most parts of the world where warm waters exist. Water hyacinth produces new plants by rapid lateral growth, and in some parts of the country, by seeds. Fragments of existing plants can also give rise to new plants. When stands of water hyacinth totally cover a pond surface several changes occur. Less oxygen diffuses into the water and more oxygen is consumed due to the mass of plant tissue that eventually drops to the bottom. Other submersed plants are eliminated due to intense shading. Water hyacinth also clogs water control structures and impedes boat traffic. In Florida, large harvesting machines are used to remove the plant from infested areas. Research is underway to find insects that might control the pest. Along the Grand Strand only a few problems with water hyacinth have been reported.

Useful for anything?

Because of its rapid growth and ability to remove nutrients from water, water hyacinth is a prime candidate for wastewater treatment. Specifically, systems have been developed where water hyacinth is grown in ponds through which wastewater is circulated. When these systems are filled with plants, the material is harvested and taken to the landfill. Such systems with biological filters are low-cost approaches to pollution control.

Getting around

Water hyacinth plants are constantly floating down the Waccamaw River and thus are dispersed throughout this freshwater system. Plants also snag on boat trailers when boats are loaded at launching ramps. The next launch site then gets a fresh supply of water hyacinth.

See also: Conway Riverwalk, Waccamaw National Wildlife Refuge, Sandy Island, storm water detention pond

Wax myrtle

Wax myrtle leaves and fruit.

As in Myrtle Beach

Wax myrtle is a multi-stemmed, evergreen shrub found in many different habitats of the Grand Strand region. It is recognized by the toothed leaves that have small orange dots on both sides. The leaves are aromatic when crushed. Female shrubs have numerous small, grey fruits produced close to the stem. The town of Myrtle Beach was named after this shrub when early settlers found extensive stands of the species near the beach.

A green pharmacy

Many herbal remedies have been produced from various parts of wax myrtle. The root and bark are harvested, ground, and sold as an antibiotic and as a treatment for inflamed mucus membranes. The Indians and early settlers made a tea of the leaves and drank it to relieve fevers and dysentery. Leaves crushed and rubbed on the skin may repel mosquitoes. Leaves placed in closed spaces such as cabinets may keep out insects. The exact reason for the many uses of wax myrtle is not known. However, the plant contains a wide variety of oils, waxes, resins, and pigments. Some of these natural products are toxic and thus herbal products derived from wax myrtle should not be used by women who are pregnant.

Those expensive candles

The fruits of wax myrtle are covered by a wax used for making bayberry candles and other products. The wax can be separated from the fruits by boiling them in water and then scraping the wax from the water surface. True bayberry candles do not smoke, producing a smell that is light and spicy.

In the landscape

Many urban areas along the Grand Strand have been landscaped with wax myrtle. The plant grows in a wide variety of soil conditions and may achieve a height of 40 feet. Visitors to the Grand Strand might pluck a few of the waxy fruits and take them home as a reminder of their vacation. After the waxy coating is rubbed off, the seeds will germinate and plants will grow in the coastal plain anywhere from New Jersey to Texas.

See also: bay trees, Myrtle Beach State Park, pine, yaupon

Yaupon

Yaupon's red berries are eaten by many types of wildlife.

What is it?

Yaupon is a large, evergreen shrub growing in several types of habitats along the Grand Strand. It is easily recognized by the dark green oval-shaped leaves (with scalloped edges) and the bright red fruits. This member of the holly family is perhaps most easily observed when it forms dense, impenetrable thickets on the backsides of sand dunes. These thickets often show dramatic salt pruning where exposed branches are eliminated and new growth occurs in pockets of air protected from the wind. Yaupon also grows as solitary individuals in maritime forests and pine forests. In forests and protected areas the plant can attain a height of 25 feet.

Can I eat it?

No. In fact the fruits are toxic to humans. However, birds do eat them and this is the primary method of seed dispersal. The young tender leaves of yaupon are notorious for their high caffeine content. Indeed, the Indians made a tea of yaupon leaves called "black drink" and this was important in various rituals. The scientific name, *Ilex vomitoria*, is derived from the historical use of the plant in cleansing ceremonies. These rituals involved vomiting---yaupon may have been associated with this effect. However, scientists now think that other plants in the tea mixture caused this unpleasant symptom. The nutrient content of yaupon leaves is relatively high and deer actively seek them out.

Yaupon in the home landscape

Because of its shiny leaves and fruit display, yaupon is planted as a border or specimen shrub around many homes along the Grand Strand. It tolerates a wide range of environmental conditions although growth is relatively slow. It has also been used as a sand stabilizer around some of the beach resorts. The plant readily sprouts from roots when it is pruned or top-killed.

On the move

Living plants and archeological remains of yaupon have been found in isolated sites far-removed from the natural range of the species. Some think that Indians transported the species to new locations. If so, this would represent one of the first examples of woody-plant horticulture.

See also: Huntington Beach State Park, Myrtle Beach State Park, sea oats, wax myrtle

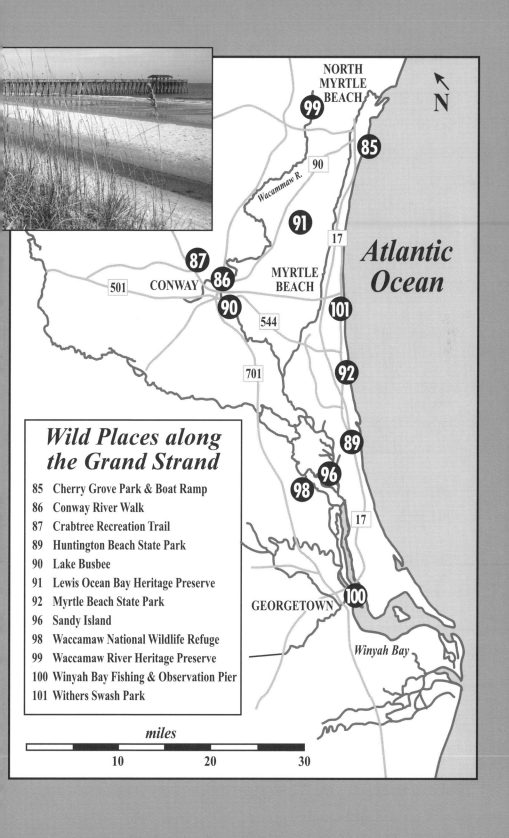

NORTH
MYRTLE
BEACH

99

85

N

90

Wacammaw R.

91

17

Atlantic
Ocean

87
86

501   CONWAY

MYRTLE
BEACH

90

544

101

701

92

Wild Places along
the Grand Strand

89

85   Cherry Grove Park & Boat Ramp

86   Conway River Walk

87   Crabtree Recreation Trail

89   Huntington Beach State Park

96

98

90   Lake Busbee

91   Lewis Ocean Bay Heritage Preserve

92   Myrtle Beach State Park

17

96   Sandy Island

98   Waccamaw National Wildlife Refuge

99   Waccamaw River Heritage Preserve

100 Winyah Bay Fishing & Observation Pier

101 Withers Swash Park

GEORGETOWN   **100**

Winyah Bay

miles

10   20   30

Carolina Bays

Photo by M. Scott Harr

Carolina Bays typically support thickets of evergreen shrubs. (above)
The distinctive oval shape of Carolina Bays is best viewed from the air. (right)

What are they?

Carolina Bays are oval depressional wetlands that occur throughout the Grand Strand. From the air, they look like giant footprints. The ends of the bays are formed by dry, elevated sand ridges. These are shallow natural wetlands that are fed primarily by rainwater. Water depth varies from bay to bay and from year to year. In some cases open water is found at the center. In other cases the bays are completely overgrown by trees and dense shrub thickets. The name "bay" comes from the presence of bay trees typically found growing in this habitat.

Mysterious origins

Carolina Bays are the subject of much scientific controversy because of their uniform shape and orientation (i.e., northwest to southeast). Some think that the bays were once (100,000 years ago) shallow lakes that eventually filled with dead plant material called peat. The more mundane explanations for shape invoke the action of wind that removes material from the centers and deposits it at the ends. The more fantastic explanations propose that bays are impact craters of meteors or spawning beds of long-extinct prehistoric fishes.

Bay basics

As unique wetlands, Carolina Bays are afforded some degree of protection. In addition to serving as massive biological filters, bays also support a wide range of plant and animal life. Specifically, dense shrub vegetation that often grows in bays is prime habitat for black bears. The edges of bays also produce some of the Grand Strands rarest and most interesting plants. Venus' fly traps grow almost exclusively at the margins of Carolina Bays. These insect trappers also occur in association with other carnivorous plants such as pitcher plants and sundews. Various orchids also are found in this habitat; some of them produce dramatic floral displays in the aftermath of fires.

A day at the bay

The best view of Carolina Bays is from the air. As you fly into or out of Myrtle Beach Airport look out the window and note these landscape features. Most will be seen within 10 miles of the beach. If you want to explore a Carolina Bay from the ground, the best place to do this is at Lewis Ocean Bay Heritage Preserve. Here you will find sparse pine plantations interspersed with bays. Bays will be recognized by the slight drop in elevation and the presence of thick impenetrable shrub vegetation. Many of the bays at Lewis Ocean Bay have been protected by fire line ditches. This is to prevent fires from igniting the peat substrate. Peat, once ignited, can burn for many months.

Threats to bays

The vast majority of Carolina Bays throughout the southeast have been altered by draining, logging, or agriculture. However, recent research suggests that Carolina Bays are critical wetlands necessary for the future viability of many types of plants and animals. Future efforts to preserve nature along the Grand Strand will likely focus on protecting bays and the organisms living in them.

See also: black bear, Lewis Ocean Bay Heritage Preserve, pitcher plant, Venus' fly trap

Cherry Grove Park and Boat Ramp 85

Cherry Grove Park and Boat Ramp offers easy access to the water near Hog Inlet on the north end of the Grand Strand.

Inshore access

Cherry Grove Park, a multi-use site maintained by the City of North Myrtle Beach, includes a launching ramp, a fishing pier, picnic shelters, and remnants of an interpretive trail. A small protected sandy beach is great for wading. The park allows access to Williams Creek and the salt marsh system connected to this creek. Admission is free.

A study in contrast

The interpretive trail at Cherry Grove Park shows aerial photographs of how this section of the Grand Strand was highly modified for housing development. A series of parallel, interconnected canals was excavated so that houses could have access to water. Indeed, such development continues to the present on a site adjacent to the park. Just a mile to the north and across Hog Inlet is Waites Island. The is one of the last undeveloped sections of the Grand Strand. It is owned and operated by Coastal Carolina University for education and research purposes. Hog Inlet serves to divide two very different beach scenes.

Barrier island ecology

Cherry Grove Park offers good glimpses of processes in operation on the back side of a barrier island. Those who like mud can easily step off into the salt marsh and see fiddler crabs and periwinkles. These animals move with the tides. The marsh is actively eroding in several places, and the extensive root systems of smooth cordgrass are visible. The berms around the canals and mounds in the salt marsh now support dense stands of red cedar, wax myrtle, groundsel bush, and marshelder. These shrubs typically grow when protected from direct salt spray and when soil mounding gets the roots above the salt water. Shrub thickets are great places to view mockingbirds, wrens, and cedar waxwings.

Getting there

Take US 17 north from North Myrtle Beach. Turn right on SC 9 and head toward the beach. Turn left on Ocean Blvd. and then go to 53rd Ave. North where you will turn left again. The park is at the end of 53rd Ave. North in Cherry Grove.

See also: blue crab, fiddler crab, mullet, oyster, salt marsh periwinkle, smooth cordgrass

Conway Riverwalk

86

The Conway Riverwalk provides an arboretum in a historical setting and is one of the best places to experience the Waccamaw River.

What is it?

The Conway Riverwalk is an elevated boardwalk that winds along the riverfront area of Conway. The area adjacent to the Riverwalk is the site of many festivals and community events. Visitors strolling the length of the Riverwalk will see the Waccamaw River as well as the forest communities that grow near the river. The Waccamaw River was historically the major route for export of pitch, tar, and other forest products. The riverfront area was at one time the center of commerce in Conway.

Why is the water black?

Don't be alarmed by the black water of the Waccamaw River. This is a natural condition that is caused by the presence of organic acids leaching from the sandy soils of the bottomland forests. A "black water" river such as the Waccamaw is slow moving and low in oxygen. It is also very susceptible to pollution. Because of low oxygen levels, fish populations in the Waccamaw River are not large, but many different species are present.

The influence of tides

The Waccamaw River at Conway is influenced by ocean tides. Look at the bald cypress trees growing along the river. If it is low tide you will be able to see tide lines at the base of the tree trunks. These are visible as the boundary between dark and light bark. When the tide rises, fish move into the bottomland forests and forage for food. However, a falling tide will force fish back into the river. Most fishermen prefer to fish the Waccamaw River during a falling tide.

Traveling up the Waccamaw

A boat ramp at the southern end of the riverfront area (Conway Marina) is open to the public. Boaters can launch here and travel for many miles up the Waccamaw River. The main channel of the river generally is deep and free of obstructions. Indeed, a large commercial riverboat makes regular trips up the river from Conway. However, reduced speeds are advised as the channel is narrow and there are many blind curves.

How do I get there?

When traveling from the beach, enter Conway on Business 501. Cross the Waccamaw River and immediately turn right. This road will take you to a parking lot and the riverfront area.

See also: bowfin, bream, largemouth bass, Waccamaw National Wildlife Refuge, Waccamaw River Heritage Preserve

Crabtree Recreation Trail 87

Crabtree Swamp Recreational Trail for walkers, joggers, bicyclists. (above)
Crabtree Swamp floods frequently in the spring. (inset)

What is it?

The Crabtree Recreation Trail is a paved path that parallels the Crabtree Canal. This trail was developed as a result of right-of-way and conservation easements obtained by the City of Conway. Hikers and bikers can gain access to the trail at several points. Over a distance of about 2 miles, the trail provides unique glimpses of a seasonally flooded bottomland forest.

What will I see?

If you enter the trail where it intersects Hwy. 701, the Crabtree Canal will be on your right and the bottomland forest will be on your left. The Crabtree Canal collects water from nearly half of the City of Conway. This water eventually flows into the Waccamaw River. The bottomland forest is interesting in that it represents the type of forest that develops when commercially important bald cypress trees are removed. If you venture into the forest notice the large cypress stumps. Although you can still find a few veteran bald cypress trees, the forest is comprised mostly of red maple, swamp chestnut oak, overcup oak, laurel oak, sweet gum, and American elm. These species emerged into dominance when the bald cypress trees were cut. In the understory you will see large individuals of dwarf palmetto, a species that thrives in wet habitats. The edge of the canal and depressions in the forest are great places to see snakes and turtles.

Why a canal?

The Crabtree Canal is an engineered structure built for the conveyance of water. Flooding was and still is a problem in Conway and in the surrounding areas. Construction of a deep and straight canal facilitated the movement of water out of the city, but such structures may actually increase flood pulses at locations farther downstream. The low elevation of Conway and its proximity to the Waccamaw River likely conspire to make flooding a common event.

How do I find it?

Take Business 501 through Conway and leave the city going west on Main Street which will eventually turn into Hwy. 701. About one mile outside of Conway the road will cross Crabtree Canal. Park near the pump station on the right side of the road and walk down to the canal. The paved trail begins at that point.

See also: bald cypress, freshwater wetland, stormwater retention pond.

95

Freshwater Wetland ⭐88

Water moves slowly through these freshwater wetlands. (above)
Several types of freshwater wetlands can often be seen side by side. (inset)

Wetlands everywhere

Because of the low elevation (i.e., low country) and the relative absence of hills or bluffs, much of the land near the Grand Strand is wetland. Wetlands are characterized by water-saturated soils and by special plants that can grow in these soils. The large area of wetland and the diversity of wetland types contributes to the great variety of wild things that live near the Grand Strand. However, wetlands also pose unique problems when development occurs. Wetlands are protected by the Clean Water Act, and thus impacts to wetlands must be avoided or mitigated.

Nature's sponge

Wetlands are protected because scientists have documented several valuable services. First, wetlands provide food, habitat, and shelter for a great variety of animals. Some of these animals are year-around residents, while others use wetlands solely for reproduction or during migration. The other important function is that wetlands filter nutrients and sediments washing from non-wetland areas. Wetlands regulate the water quality in streams, rivers, and oceans. Because of their filtering abilities, wetlands have been used to treat polluted waters before they are released into streams.

Our freshwater wetlands

Along the Grand Strand one can identify the following wetland types: Carolina bay, bottomland forest, tidal river marsh, tidal bottomland forest and non-tidal marsh. Carolina bays are depression wetlands where water is supplied primarily by rainfall. These may dry out in the summer and are susceptible to wild fires. Bottomland forests occur near rivers and are prone to seasonal flooding, but they are not so close to rivers that they have tidal influence. They may be dry at some times of the year. Tidal river marshes (no trees but lots of cattail, wild rice, and common reed) and tidal bottomland forests (mostly bald cypress and tupelo) occur along all major rivers of the Grand Strand. The water regimen here is primarily determined by river flow and daily tidal fluctuation. Non-tidal marshes may develop in stagnant areas where drainage is impeded. Storm-water detention ponds often develop into non-tidal marshes when water is less than a foot deep. These usually emerge as cattail marshes.

See also: bald cypress, Carolina bay, Crabtree Recreation Trail, pickerel weed, water hyacinth

Huntington Beach State Park

A boardwalk leads out into the salt marsh. (above)
Atalaya Castle is a popular attraction at Huntington Beach State Park. (inset)

What is it?

Huntington Beach State Park located 3 miles south of Murrell's Inlet on US 17 is perhaps the premier site along the Grand Strand for viewing and enjoying nature. This area (and Brookgreen Gardens) was once the private preserve of Archer Milton Huntington and his wife Anna Hyatt Huntington. Anna Huntington was a sculptress; her influence is obvious in the design of the winter home, Atalaya, that still exists at the south end of the park. The Huntington's recognized the unique ecological features of this site. The original purchase of the land in 1930 was to provide a site for fishing, hunting, and nature study. Today, the park and its 2500 acres of beach, salt marsh, freshwater lagoon and maritime forest, and campground is operated by the state of South Carolina.

Little effort; big rewards

Visitors with children will appreciate the layout of the park and its accessible features. This is the one place on the Grand Strand where alligators can be consistently seen from a car on the causeway. An education center is located at the start of the marsh boardwalk. Here one can learn about salt marsh ecology; a bird viewing area even provides binoculars for visitor use. A short walk on the marsh boardwalk will reveal periwinkles, fiddler crabs, and mud minnows.

Hiking into nature

For those who wish to stretch their legs and get close to nature, two trails are available. The Kerrigan Nature Trail starting behind the park office takes you through maritime forest and eventually leads to platforms overlooking the freshwater lagoon. The Sandpiper Pond Nature Trail begins at the north parking lot for the jetty. It takes you through dense thickets of wax myrtle and eventually leads to sites where one can view a brackish pond. Both the freshwater lagoon and the brackish pond are prime birding areas where one can see waterfowl and shorebirds.

To the jetty

Serious nature watchers and fishermen must hike to the jetty. Follow the signs to the jetty parking lot and then take the boardwalk to the beach. Turn left and start walking. You can see the jetty far in distance. It is about 1.5 miles to your destination so make sure to pack water and some snacks. Fishermen making this trek have fashioned a wide variety of wagons and carts for transferring their equipment. This section of the beach will reveal shorebirds and dolphin. About halfway to the jetty the dunes have been leveled by large waves. Behind this overwash area is a large lagoon that is an important nesting area for terns and shorebirds. The jetty has a paved flat top so walking is easy. At low tide red and green algae are visible. Sea turtles can often be observed swimming along the rocks. Fishermen here catch bluefish, flounder, spot tail bass, spots, pinfish, and croakers.

See also: American alligator, bottlenose dolphin, fiddler crab, ghost crab, great egret, gull, sea-oats, seaweed

Lake Busbee

A variety of freshwater wetlands can be seen around Lake Busbee. (above)

Lake Busbee and the power plant. (inset)

A lake near the river

Lake Busbee is a 500-acre impoundment near Conway. The Santee Cooper power generating-facility pulls cooling water from the Waccamaw River. The warm water is discharged into Lake Busbee, allowing the water to cool before it is released back into the Waccamaw River. Broad and shallow, Lake Busbee, is by far the largest lake in the Grand Strand region. A low dike topped with a gravel road surrounds the entire lake, thus allowing easy access to a diverse wetland system. The area is free and open to the public, but no motorized vehicles are allowed.

The lake

Lake Busbee has several important features that attract a wide variety of water birds. It has large populations of shad. These baitfish are pursued by gulls, cormorants, great blue herons, and great egrets. Several low islands in the middle of the lake serve as gathering points for mallards, grebes, and Canada geese.

The marsh and swamp

Although the lake proper has little aquatic vegetation, the surrounding area includes canals, freshwater marshes, and swamp forests. An extensive freshwater marsh dominated by cattails has developed where trees were removed under the power lines. A turtle-filled lagoon ringed by marsh exists beyond the south end of the lake. Numerous wood duck nesting boxes in this lagoon make wood ducks a common sight. The swamp forests are mostly dominated by red maple and bald cypress. The canal system is deep and is conducive to a large variety of aquatic plants. A walk along the dike allows one to see all of these habitats and also the edges of these habitats where birds and reptiles are most active.

Beavers at work

About halfway around the lake, beavers have dammed the canal, thus impounding water in a small section of swamp forest. Here one can see numerous trees that died as a result of constant inundation. A beaver den is clearly visible and gnaw marks on the trees are common.

Getting there

Lake Busbee can only be accessed near where Church Street in Conway merges with SC 501 South. Traveling from Myrtle Beach on SC 501 North, follow the signs to SC 701 South. Proceed on SC 701 but look immediately for the sign directing you back on SC 501 South toward Myrtle Beach. This is Church Street. Go down Church Street and then park on the left side of the road. An orange metal gate marks the beginning of the hike around the lake.

See also: bald cypress, beaver, Canada goose, double-crested cormorant, great blue heron, gull

Old pine plantations are common at Lewis Ocean Bay Heritage Preserve. (above)
The sundew is the smallest common carnivorous plant. (inset)

Notable but little known

Lewis Ocean Bay Heritage Preserve is a 9000-acre tract of land between SC 90 and the Intracoastal Waterway. It is owned and managed by the State of South Carolina. The preserve is free and open to the public, but access is not well marked and the preserve is not widely publicized. Lewis Ocean Bay includes 20 relatively intact Carolina Bays surrounded by pine plantations. This is the largest preserved collection of bay habitats in the state.

A garden of unique plants

Lewis Ocean Bay provides opportunities for seeing some of the world's most fascinating plants. With a short hike along the dirt roads that cross the preserve one can see carnivorous plants such as sundews, pitcher plants, the Venus' fly trap, and butterworts. Rare orchids dot the landscape during spring and early summer. Several species of peat mosses grow in wet areas and may in some places form hummocks reminiscent of northern bogs. Carolina bays support thick and nearly impenetrable stands of shrubs and bay trees while on higher and drier sand ridges there are relatively open and stunted forests of turkey oak. There is also a restored longleaf pine forest in the middle of the preserve.

Fire in the landscape

Lewis Ocean Bay Heritage Preserve is divided into fire management units and prescribed burns occur every several years. The fires are set in order to clear out and control the fast-growing shrubs. Many of the smaller rare plants that occur in the preserve cannot survive unless the aggressive shrubs are periodically burned back to the ground. Burning also creates a suitable seedbed for rare plants to establish. However, most of the plants in the preserve are adapted to burning and within a few weeks after a fire regrowth is widespread.

The hidden animals

This is the place where at least 20 black bears can find good habitat. They live in the bays and are seldom seen. Endangered red-cockaded woodpeckers also live here, building their nests in standing dead pine trees.

How do I get there?

Take SC 90 out of Conway heading toward North Myrtle Beach. Go about 9 miles and then turn right on International Road. Another 3 miles down that road there will be a small sign that indicates the boundary of the preserve. Beware of ticks and rattlesnakes.

See also: bay tree, black bear, Carolina bay, peat moss, pine, Venus' fly trap

Myrtle Beach State Park

Myrtle Beach State Park, near the heart of Myrtle Beach SC.

What is it?

Myrtle Beach State Park, located 3 miles south of the Myrtle Beach Airport on Business 17, is a small (300-acre) tract of preserved nature now surrounded on all sides by coastal development. The park and many of its facilities were built in the 1930's by the Civilian Conservation Corps. For a brief time during World War II the park was a military base formed as a defense against possible invasion. Although not as rich in natural diversity as Huntington Beach State Park, Myrtle Beach State Park does offer some fine examples of the ecological communities that once existed throughout the Grand Strand. Indeed, part of the park has been designated as a South Carolina Heritage Trust Site. A campground, cabins, fishing pier, and a small interpretive center are found at the park. **Picnics under the oaks**

Myrtle Beach State Park is perhaps the best place on the Grand Strand where one can have a picnic and still be protected from the intense summer sun. A large stand of live oaks draped with Spanish moss extends from the park interior to the edge of the beach. Picnic tables have been placed under these oaks. Picnic shelters with nearby playgrounds are also available. Not surprisingly, the picnic area is crowded on weekends, but even on a pleasant Sunday afternoon the hustle at Myrtle Beach State Park is calm compared to the beach scene that exists outside the park boundaries.

To the maritime (or seaside) forest

Across from the large picnic shelter in the middle of the park is the beginning of the Sculptured Oak Nature Trail. This trail takes you through one of the few remaining stands of maritime forest. These forests support a unique assemblage of trees and shrubs that can persist in an environment influenced by salt spray and the occasional devastation of a hurricane. The shrub layer is thick and is dominated by evergreen species such as wax myrtle, yaupon, and bush palmetto. Large specimens of live oak, southern magnolia, and loblolly pine can be easily observed. One spur of the trail ends at a small freshwater pond and wetland system. Great blue herons and other wading birds are always found here. Hikers using this trail during the warmer months should take precautions against ticks. The best approach is to wear boots and long socks that can be pulled over the pant cuffs. Also, light-colored clothing makes it easier to see and remove ticks if they get on you.

Cut by the wind

As you emerge from the forest and head toward the beach you will see large clumps of shrubs that appear misshapen. This is yaupon and the strange form is the result of what is called salt pruning. Plant tissues exposed to wind and salt are killed and thus through time, the shrub assumes the shape defined by protected air space. The sand dunes in front of the shrubs provide protection from wind pruning.

Beach features

The fishing pier (free access for non-fishers) is a fine place to take in an unobstructed view of the sunset. In fall, dolphins can be seen chasing baitfish not far off the beach. Fishing piers are also great places to see some creatures that do swim in the shallow water of the surf zone. Expect to watch as fishermen reel in croakers, spots, pinfish, founder, sea trout, pompano, bluefish, crabs, and the occasional shark (although shark fishing is illegal).

See also: live oak, sand dunes, sea oats, Huntington Beach State Park

Rice Field

Historical rice fields now support marsh vegetation and many species of birds and wildlife. (above)
Trunks allow managers to manipulate water levels in rice fields. (inset)

What are they?

Rice fields are areas that were historically used for the production of rice as an export crop. The growing of rice in the Grand Strand area was concentrated in tidal swamps and marshes along the Waccamaw River. Indeed, this crop and the slave labor used to grow the crop made possible the development of a rich and prosperous plantation culture in the Waccamaw Neck region and in the areas surrounding Georgetown. The plantation culture peaked in the mid 1800's. However, with the loss of slave labor after the Civil War the system of rice growing could not be sustained. By the early 1900's rice production along the Grand Strand had all but ceased. Most abandoned rice fields are now privately owned and are managed as hunting preserves.

Growing with the tides

The current status of abandoned rice fields as nature preserves is closely linked to how the land was modified for the growing of rice. Many thousands of acres of swamp forest were cleared and burned. Then the land was banked and ditched to allow a tidal system of water control. Built into the banks were complex wooden structures called trunks that allowed water to flow in during high tides but also allowed water to be impounded on the rice fields when the tides fell. The ability to passively regulate water in the fields was critical to rice growth and harvest.

Abandoned rice fields get wild

There is an ongoing debate about how historical rice fields should be managed. Decay, erosion, and hurricanes have worn gaps in the banks thus allowing free exchange of water as the tide rises and falls. Repair of the water control structures is not possible due to legal restrictions. Banks in the rice fields have been colonized by bald cypress and gum trees. However, the fields proper are often marshes dominated by cattails, wild rice, and common reed. Not surprisingly, these areas attract a high diversity of waterfowl, wading birds, and other wildlife.

A view of the fields

Historical rice fields are best appreciated from a boat. Put in at the Hagley Landing on the Waccamaw River directly west of Pawley's Island. Motor across the river and go up Jericho Creek. This will take you through thousands of acres of historical rice fields and will also eventually lead to the Pee Dee River. If you don't have a boat, then go to the Winyah Bay Fishing and Observation Pier in Georgetown. Your view from the pier will reveal marshes that once supported the plantation culture. Brookgreen Gardens maintains a demonstration rice field and an interpretive center devoted to the rice culture.

See also: bald cypress, freshwater marsh, Sandy Island, Winyah Bay Fishing and Observation Pier

Salt marsh

94

Mud flats are exposed at low tide. (top)   Salt marsh behind Waites Island at high tide. (bottom)

From the land to the ocean

Along the Grand Strand, salt marshes are found in protected areas on the back sides of barrier islands. These marshes are characterized by inflows of freshwater from the land, inflow and outflow of salt water due to tidal fluctuation, complex systems of shallow tidal creeks, and extensive areas of mud colonized by smooth cordgrass. Many organisms live year around in the marshes. However, many more organisms require salt marshes as spawning habitat or as places where juveniles can pass through critical life stages. Human impacts to salt marshes can extend well beyond the boundaries of the salt marsh system.

Sorted by salt

Within a salt marsh system, variation in tidal flushing can have dramatic effects on plant communities. Smooth cordgrass adjacent to tidal creeks grows tall because the constant flushing reduces salt accumulation and also brings in nitrogen. Areas far from the tidal creeks get flushed less frequently and thus salts accumulate and nutrients are in short supply. In these areas we find salt tolerant plants such as glasswort and short forms of smooth cordgrass. Mounds of sediment may be isolated from the saltwater, thus allowing growth of shrubs such as wax myrtle and red-cedar.

Seeking structure

The larval and juvenile forms of many marine creatures live and grow in the salt marsh. Structure, the critical habitat, is provided by two key organisms: smooth cordgrass and the oyster. Smooth cordgrass produces a dense tangle of stems, leaves, and roots. This structure is available for use during most but not all tidal conditions. Oysters grow in beds and the accumulation of shell also provides structure. Oyster beds are under water most of the time and thus can be used for protection by various animals except during extremely low tides.

Protecting the marshes

Humans and their activities have a large variety of impacts in salt marshes. Most important is the change in water quantity and water quality. Development, shoreline alteration, and the increase in roads and parking lots lead to rapid runoff of stormwater. Flood events can erode the salt marsh and can also lead to increased sediment deposition. Nutrient inputs can lead to excessive algal growth and changes in the habitat quality of salt marshes. All communities along the Grand Strand are taking steps to assure that salt marshes are buffered from the impacts of increasing development. However, the constant presence of dredging operations suggests that more can be done to protect these critical ecosystems.

See also: blue crab, Cherry Grove Park and Boat Ramp, fiddler crab, Huntington Beach State Park, oyster, smooth cordgrass

Sand Dunes

Sea oats always produces a lot of seed. (above)

Foredune areas support sea oats; backdune regions support thickets of wax myrtle and other shrubs. (top)

Sea oats trap sand and build dunes. (far right)

Just off the beach

Sand dunes are berms that form along the backside of the beach typically above the highest tide. Much work has been devoted to understanding and protecting dunes simply because they defend buildings and structures from winds and waves. Dunes add some level of stability to a very unstable environment. For this reason dunes and the plants that grow on dunes should not be disturbed.

Getting a dune

The birth of a sand dune requires some kind of an object that stops or slows the wind. The object could be a plant stem or it could be an abandoned boat. When the wind is blocked this creates a place for blowing sand to accumulate. Once a dune is started, the dune itself can block the wind and thus dunes grow and change through time. Picket fences have been used to initiate dune formation but plants such as sea-oats are more commonly cultivated as dune formers. Ghost crabs build their burrows in sand dunes; it is unknown how this burrowing contributes to dune formation.

Forward, middle, and back

The fore dune or front edge of a dune is a harsh environment subject to wind, salt spray, and occasional wave action. Sea oats, sea rocket and the rare sea beach amaranth can tolerate these conditions, but most other plants can not. However, in the swales between dunes and on the back side of the dune there is some protection from the elements and thus we find other species such as yaupon which forms dense thickets.

Washing out

When hurricanes or storms occur the ocean can surge against and in some cases over the dune area. These overwash events lead to erosion and thus dune formation must be reinitiated. An excellent dune system exists at Huntington Beach State Park. Walking along the beach toward the jetty one can see relatively stable dunes as well as areas where past storms have removed the dune system. Although dunes are encouraged as a way of protecting beachfront property, the loose sand of the dune/beach system is inherently unstable and will always be in a condition of change controlled by wind and waves.

See also: Huntington Beach State Park, sea oats, sea rocket, yaupon

Sandy Island

Primitive trails on Sandy Island offer easy hiking. (above)
Edges of Sandy Island support dense cyrpress swamps. (inset)

What is it?

Sandy Island is a 9000-acre nature preserve located between the Waccamaw and Great Pee Dee Rivers. The preserve represents one of the largest tracts of undeveloped freshwater island ecosystems in the eastern United States. Protection of Sandy Island in 1997 came about as a result of several unrelated events. First, the South Carolina Department of Transportation (SCDOT) was required to mitigate environmental impacts associated with the many road-building projects around the Grand Strand. In short, the SCDOT needed to acquire tracts that would compensate for wetlands lost to road projects. At about this time, the owners of Sandy Island were considering construction of a bridge that would open the area to development. Fearing that such development would lead to loss of many unique biological, geological, and archeological resources, a coalition of public and private organizations was formed and the work began to craft a land purchase. Eventually the majority of the island was purchased by the SCDOT. The bridge to the island was not built and Sandy Island now represents a gem of protected nature that few people ever visit.

Who lives there?

There are about 100 permanent residents living on the south end of Sandy Island. Many of the people who live there are related to slaves that once worked in the rice plantations prior to the Civil War. Access to the island is by boat. The residents, many of which work on the Grand Strand, commute via the Sandy Island Landing. The only school boat in South Carolina ferries children from Sandy Island to schools in surrounding area.

Why is Sandy Island interesting?

In contrast to most of the Grand Strand, Sandy Island has a variety of topographical features ranging from low wetlands to raised sandy bluffs. There are two trails on the island and in one a short walk one can see tidal freshwater marshes, forested wetlands, maritime forests, and longleaf pine forests. The South Carolina chapter of The Nature Conservancy manages many of these ecosystems by prescribed burning. Bears, ospreys, turkeys, and even endangered red-cockaded woodpeckers can be found. The great variety of ecosystems means that nature photographers can find good subjects almost year round. Several dozen archeological sites have been identified where one can see vestiges of the plantation culture.

Making the trip.

You need a boat to get to this great place and you need to make some preparations. Bring food, water, and bug repellent. The best approach is via the Wacca Wache Landing at the end of Wachesaw Road. The landing is marked by a sign on U.S. Highway 17 in Murrell's Inlet. Launch your boat and head north up the Waccamaw River. Turn left at the first major tributary entering the Waccamaw River (Big Bull Creek) and proceed about 1 mile to Little Bull Creek which will be on your left. About 25 yards before Little Bull Creek look for a small opening in the shoreline vegetation and the remnants of a boat dock. This is it. Beach your boat and proceed to the sign that describes the nature trail.

See also: longleaf pine, freshwater wetland, rice field, Waccamaw National Wildlife Refuge

Stormwater Detention Ponds

Stormwater detention ponds offer habitat for many plants and animals.

What are they?
You've probably noticed that all the shopping centers and housing complexes in Myrtle Beach are surrounded by bodies of water: long ditches, small ponds, and large lakes. These storm water detention ponds are now required by law when large areas of land are paved. Rain water falling on parking lots is channeled into the detention ponds. The water is temporarily stored until it can slowly sink into the ground or gradually flow into local streams.

Why are they required by law?
The Grand Strand is a low, flat area that is naturally susceptible to flooding. As more and more of the land gets paved, more and more water is directed as surface flow, creating local floods when torrential rains occur. Storm water detention ponds are not a perfect solution to the runoff problem, but they do help.

Why are retention ponds neat places?
Wetlands are prominent natural features of the Grand Strand environment. That also means that we have an abundance of plants and animals that live in wetlands. Storm water detention ponds are quickly occupied by all kinds of creatures. They are great wildlife viewing areas with easy access. You can see yellow-bellied sliders, eastern cottonmouth, bream, mosquito fish, herons, and egrets.

Where are the best ones?
Clear water with lots of plant growth. That's the right combination for seeing the pond fauna. Start with the retention ditch surrounding the Food Lion plaza 1/2 mile east of the Coastal Carolina University sign on Rt. 501. This ditch often resembles a giant aquarium where you can watch yellow-bellied sliders bumping into bream. Barefoot Landing is built over one large storm water detention lake. The yellow-bellied sliders there are addicted to food pellets, but the birds hiding in cattails should not be missed. Watch your step, however. It is not uncommon for alligators to claim isolated detention ponds as their own.

See also: freshwater wetland, great blue heron, great egret, pickerel weed, yellow-bellied slider

Waccamaw National Wildlife Refuge 98

Small creeks offer the opportunity to explore the refuge. (above)
Bald cypress forests dominate the edges of the river. (inset)

What is it?

The Waccamaw National Wildlife Refuge (WNWR) is the Grand Strand's most recently designated nature preserve under the jurisdiction of the U.S. Fish and Wildlife Service. The refuge is located adjacent to Sandy Island and includes lands bordering the Waccamaw, Great Pee Dee, and Little Pee Dee Rivers. Currently the WNWR occupies about 7000 acres, but it will grow to nearly 50,000 acres. It will eventually be a major site for the preservation of wetland habitats critical to populations of migratory and resident birds.

What does it look like?

Access to the refuge is by boat. Visitors will not find improved landings or trails. This place is strictly for nature. However, simply cruising the edges of the swamp forest will likely be rewarding for photographers, nature watchers, and day trippers. On a typical day one can see osprey perched in the large veteran bald cypress trees that occur sporadically at the margins. Alligators will be moving slowly in the backwater areas. Canoeists and kayakers can paddle into the small creeks that once formed the water control system associated with rice fields. If you are quiet, various warbler species can be seen in the shrubs bordering the swamp forest. As the waters fall due to tidal influence, fiddler crabs can be seen scurrying in the mud flats that support a fringing emergent wetland community. In early spring, flowering wild azaleas can form a nearly solid wall of color at the forest edge.

Is the fishing any good?

The WNWR is an excellent place to combine fishing with nature watching. This is a blackwater system and fishing is best in spring when the bream become active. Locals stick with the basics: a long cane pole baited with crickets or red worms. Move slowly along the riverbank and drop your bait in small pockets or cuts. Downed trees are also great fish attractors. If you can find a place where bream are congregated, then you will also likely catch a fair number of crappie mixed in with the bream. Try small (1/16 ounce) jigs under these conditions. In these waters bass fishing is unpredictable, but bowfins (caught using bass tactics) are great fun.

How do I get there?

From Myrtle Beach travel south on Highway 17. Across from Murrells Inlet look for the signs to the Wacca Wache Landing. Turn right on Wachesaw Road. This will take you to the landing. Go north (to your right) up the Waccamaw River about 1.5 miles and then turn left on the first major tributary, Bull Creek. Travel about 1 mile on Bull Creek and look for a small tributary on the left (Little Bull Creek). Little Bull Creek forms the southern boundary of the WNWR. You will see the signs. One can stay on Bull Creek and eventually enter the Great Pee Dee River.

See also: Alligator, bald cypress, freshwater wetland, osprey, rice field, Sandy Island

Waccamaw River Heritage Preserve

One of the newest Heritage Preserves in the region.

For paddlers only

The Waccamaw River Heritage Preserve includes 5000 acres of land adjacent to a 30-mile stretch of the Waccamaw River. Access is free and the preserve is open to the public year around. However, most of the area can be experienced only while floating down the river. This section of the Waccamaw makes numerous twists and turns. Plenty of opportunities exist for exploring sloughs off of the main channel.

What will I see?

This is wild country where many species of birds, reptiles, and mammals live. The predominant vegetation is bottomland forest. Warblers, wood ducks, barred owls, and pileated woodpeckers are common. Black bears occasionally use this preserve as a migration route. Otters and beavers may be seen while paddling at dusk. Snakes and turtles are abundant, and one should be aware of eastern cottonmouths along the shore.

Where does the water come from?

Water in the Waccamaw River originates from Lake Waccamaw, a Carolina Bay lake in North Carolina. This is a blackwater river rich in organic acids leached from the peaty soils of the bottomlands. Aerial photos suggest that the channel of the Waccamaw River is constantly on the move. When flood waters erode the banks on tight turns, the channel may eventually move, leaving a slough where once flowed a river. Many sandbars along the river indicate active processes of erosion and deposition.

How do I get there?

Six landings provide access to the river. The water trail officially begins at Wortham's Ferry Landing. To get there, drive west on SC 9 and turn right on SC 57. Drive 2 miles and turn left on country road 111. The landing is at the end of this road. When on the river, expect travel speeds of 2-4 mph.

See also: bald cypress, black bear, bowfin, bream, Waccamaw National Wildlife Refuge

Winyah Bay Fishing & Observation Pier

The old road bridge has been utilized as the Winyah Bay Fishing and Observation Pier and offers good views as well as fishing access.

A place for seeing the big picture

The Winyah Bay Fishing and Observation Pier is a relatively new recreational site owned and operated by the City of Georgetown. The pier was developed from an old and incomplete bridge that once crossed the Great Pee Dee River. One segment of the bridge is open to the public 7 days a week. No admission fee is charged. The pier offers visitors what is perhaps the best sweeping view of Winyah Bay and the marshes surrounding the bay.

A place where waters meet

Winyah Bay is an incredible place where nature happens in big ways. Four major rivers end at or near the bay: Sampit, Black, Great Pee Dee, and the Waccamaw. Nearly 70,000 acres of land drain into this system. It is an intimidating place for boaters because of the sometimes violent mixing of fresh and salt water, perpetual winds, and the large area. Still, Winyah Bay offers one of the best places along the southeast coast to see and experience estuaries and the organisms they support.

The legacy of rice

The pier is surrounded by marshlands that once were devoted to the cultivation of rice. Rice no longer grows here, and the water control structures associated with rice fields are mostly destroyed, but the effects of rice culture are still evident. These marshes have been mostly colonized by common reed, an invasive species that thrives in disturbed areas. There is little evidence that bald cypress swamps that once occupied these sites are coming back. Indeed, recent droughts allowed more salt water to push into the rivers, thus killing or stunting many of the trees that could have initiated forest development.

Good fishing; good views

The pier offers excellent opportunities for seeing both shorebirds and marsh birds. At some times of the year fishing is good for catfish, croakers, flounder, and red drum. Blue crabs are abundant. Bottlenose dolphins will occasionally pass by the pier as they follow fish up the Great Pee Dee River.

Getting there

Take US 17 south from Myrtle Beach toward Georgetown. The first bridge outside of Georgetown crosses the Waccamaw River. The second bridge crosses the Great Pee Dee. As you cross this bridge the pier is visible on the right. Soon after crossing the Great Pee Dee look for the sign and turn right. Follow this road to the pier.

See also: bald cypress, common reed, Atlantic croaker, bottlenose dolphin, flounder, red drum, rice field

Withers Swash Park 101

The dock offers good views of the wetlands and Myrtle Beach amusements. (above)
Withers Swash Park has well developed trails. (inset)

A park in the city

Withers Swash Park is a public natural and recreational area maintained by the City of Myrtle Beach. It is located amid the downtown hustle just a few blocks from the beach. With picnic facilities, a playground, walking trails, and a lagoon overlook, this park is well suited for families seeking an afternoon away from the sun and the beach. There is no admission fee.

What's a swash?

An area where storm water drains into the ocean is called a "swash". There are several of these along the Grand Strand. There is indeed a swash associated with Withers Swash Park, but the park itself is built along a catchment lagoon several blocks from the actual swash. During periods of intense rain, water quality in swashes can be low due to runoff from residential and commercial areas. The tidal lagoon temporarily holds water coming from the city, allowing sediments to fall out and thus providing some improvement in water quality. The lagoon also provides unique wildlife habitat.

For the birds

The covered lagoon overlook is a wonderful place to sit and observe both marsh and shore birds. Proximity to the beach means that gulls and sanderlings mix with herons and egrets. These quiet wild things can be observed with a roller coaster forming the background of the scene.

Nature next to people

At one end of Withers Swash Park is a demonstration Residential Ecosystem. Here various tree species have been planted to show what will and will not grow in the sandy soils close to the beach. The park itself is a forest of loblolly pine and water oak with occasional smaller specimens of live oak. The lagoon has tidal influence and thus the vegetation is smooth cordgrass and needle rush. There is a network of tidal creeks and some mud flat areas.

Getting there

From downtown Myrtle Beach, drive south on Business 17. Turn right on 3rd Ave. South and go one block. Look for the park sign and turn left on Withers Swash Drive. Parking is along Withers Swash Drive.

See also: Great blue heron, great egret, live oak, pine, salt marsh, smooth cordgrass, storm water detention pond

About the Authors

James Luken is a Professor in the Department of Biology at Coastal Carolina University. He teaches ecology and studies rare plants associated with Carolina Bays.

Richard Moore is a Professor in the Department of Biology at Coastal Carolina University where he serves as Assistant Vice President for Grants and Sponsored Research. He teaches ichthyology and studies fishes.

101 Wild Things Scientific Names

Animals

acorn barnacle (*Chthamalus fragilis*)
American alligator (*Alligator mississippiensis*)
Atlantic croaker (*Micropogonias undulatus*)
Atlantic menhaden (*Brevoortia tyrannus*)
Atlantic oyster drill (*Urosalpinx cinerea*)
Atlantic starfish (*Asterias forbesi*)
beaver (*Castor canadensis*)
blue crab (*Callinectes sapidus*)
bluefish (*Pomatomus saltatrix*)
bluegill (*Lepomis macrochirus*)
bottlenose dolphin (*Tursiops truncatus*)
broad-headed skink (*Eumeces laticeps*)
bowfin (*Amia calva*)
brown pelican (*Pelecanus occidentalis*)
brown shrimp (*Farfantepenaeus aztecus*)
cannonball jelly (*Stomolophus meleagris*)
Canada goose (*Branta canadensis*)
coquina (*Donax variabilis*)
deer fly (*Chrysops spp.*)
deer tick (*Ixodes scapularis*)
double-crested cormorant (*Phalacrocorax auritus*)
eastern cottonmouth (*Agkistrodon piscivorus*)
eastern oyster (*Crassostrea virginica*)
finger sponge (*Haliclona oculata*)
flathead catfish (*Pylodictis olivaris*)
ghost crab (*Ocypode quadrata*)
great blue heron (*Ardea herodias*)
great egret (*Ardea albus*)
green anole (*Anolis carolinensis*)
hard clam (*Mercenaria mercenaria*)
herring gull (*Larus argentatus*)
horse fly (*Tabanus spp.*)
horseshoe crab (*Limulus polyphemus*)
incongruous ark (*Anadara brasiliana*)
knobbed whelk (*Busycon carica*)
laughing gull (*Larus atricilla*)
lettered olive (*Oliva sayana*)
largemouth bass (*Micropterus salmoides*)
lion's mane jelly (*Cyanea capillata*)
loggerhead sea turtle (*Caretta caretta*)
lone star tick (*Amblyomma americanum*)
moon jellyfish (*Aurelia aurita*)
moon snail (*Polinices duplicatus*)
mosquito fish (*Gambusia holbrooki*)
mud fiddler crab (*Uca pugnax*)
mud minnow (*Fundulus heteroclitus*)

mushroom jelly (*Rhopilema verrilli*)
osprey (*Pandion halaetus*)
pinfish (*Lagodon rhomboides*)
pink shrimp (*Farfantepenaeus duorarum*)
Portuguese man-of-war (*Physalia physalis*)
pumpkinseed (*Lepomis gibbosus*)
red drum (*Sciaenops ocellatus*)
redbreast sunfish (*Lepomis auritus*)
redear sunfish (*Lepomis microlophus*)
red-jointed fiddler crab (*Uca minax*)
rigid pen shell (*Atrina rigida*)
ring-billed gull (*Larus delawarensis*)
sanderling (*Calidris alba*)
sand fiddler crab (*Uca pugilator*)
saw-tooth pen shell (*Atrina serrata*)
sea nettle (*Chrysaora quinquecirrha*)
sea wasp (*Chiropsalmus quadrumanus*)
southern flounder (*Paralichthys lethostigma*)
southern stingray (*Dasyatis americana*)
spot (*Leiostomus xanthurus*)
spotted sunfish (*Lepomis punctatus*)
spotted seatrout (*Cynoscion nebulosus*)
striped mullet (*Mugil cephalus*)
white ibis (*Eudocimus albus*)
white shrimp (*Litopenaeus setiferus*)
willet (*Catoptrophorus semipalmatus*)
wood duck (*Aix sponsa*)
yellow-bellied slider turtle (*Trachemys scripta*)

Plants

bald cypress (*Taxodium distichum*)
cabbage palmetto (*Sabal palmetto*)
common reed (*Phragmites australis*)
dwarf palmetto (*Sabal minor*)
firewheel (*Gaillardia pulchella*)
glasswort (*Salicornia virginica*)
gulfweed (*Sargassum spp.*)
live oak (*Quercus virginiana*)
loblolly pine (*Pinus taeda*)
longleaf pine (*Pinus palustris*)
peat moss (*Sphagnum spp.*)
pickerel weed (*Pontedaria cordata*)
pitcher plant (*Sarracenia spp.*)
poison ivy (*Toxicodendron radicans*)
sandspur (*Cenchrus tribuloides*)
sea lettuce (*Ulva spp.*)

sea rocket (*Cakile edentula*)
smooth cordgrass (*Spartina alterniflora*)
Spanish moss (*Tillandsia usneoides*)
switchcane (*Arundinaria gigantea*)
Venus' fly trap (*Dionaea muscipula*)
water hyacinth (*Eichhornia crassipes*)
wax myrtle (*Myrica cerifera*)
yaupon (*Ilex vomitoria*)

References Used in this Book and Resources for More Information

Amos, W.H. and S. H. Amos. 1985. Atlantic and Gulf Coasts. Alfred A. Knopf, Inc., New York.

Chesapeake Bay Program, Animals and Plants. 2003. http://www.chesapeakebay.net/baybio

Edwards, A. L. 1997. Georgia's sea shells. University of Georgia. http://www.arches.uga.edu/~amylyne/GSC/seashellGA

Georgia Museum of Natural History and Georgia Department of Natural Resources, Georgia Wildlife Web Site. 2000. http://naturalhistory.uga.edu/gawildlife/gaww

Gough, G.A., J.R. Sauer, and M. Iliff. 1998. Patuxent Bird Identification Infocenter. Version 97.1. Patuxent Wildlife Research Center, Laurel, MD. http:mbr-pwrc.usgs.gov/infocenter/infocenter

Gosner, K.L. 1978. A Field Guide to the Atlantic Seashore. Houghton Mifflin Co., Boston, MA.

Porcher, R.D. and D.A. Rayner. 2001. A guide to the wildflowers of South Carolina. University of South Carolina Press, Columbia, SC.

Russell, A.B. 1997. Trees of the Maritime Forest. Consumer Horticulture Fact Sheets. http://www.ces.ncsu.edu/depts./hort/consumer/facsheets/maritime.

Savannah River Ecology Lab, University of Georgia, Environmental Outreach Publications. 2001. http:www.uga.edu/srel

Smithsonian Marine Station at Fort Pierce, Species Reports. 2001. http://www.sms.si.edu/irlspec/Species_Rpts

South Carolina Department of Natural Resources and NOAA Coastal Services Center, Ace Basin Species Gallery. 2001. http:///www.csc.noaa.gov/acebasin/specgal

South Carolina Department of Natural Resources, Heritage Trust Program Preserve Guide. 2001. http://dnr.state.sc.us/wild/heritage/hp

South Carolina Department of Natural Resources, Sea Science Series. 2003. http://www.dnr/state.sc.us/marine/pub/seascience

Spitsbergen, J.M. 1980. Seacoast Life, An Ecological Guide to Natural Seashore Communities of North Carolina. The University of North Carolina Press, Chapel Hill, NC.

University of Florida Institute of Food and Agricultural Sciences and Florida Department of Agriculture and Consumer Services, Featured Creatures, http://creatures.ifas.ufl.edu/